UNDER THE GREEN BANNERS

UNDER THE GREEN BANNERS

The story of a season, the season of a lifetime

BY

NEIL K. WARNER

Photos by Troy Verde

CFI

Springville, Utah

ISBN: 1-55517-754-9
e. 1

Published by Bonneville Books
Imprint of Cedar Fort Inc.
www.cedarfort.com

Distributed by:

Typeset by Natalie K. Roach
Cover design by Nicole Cunningham

Printed in the United States of America
10 9 8 7 6 5 4 3 2 1

Printed on acid-free paper

DEDICATION

For David and R. J.
No matter how long you're gone,
your influence lives on and on.

TABLE OF CONTENTS

FOREWORD

Inevitably when a group of old men gather, the conversation will always turn to "When we were young."

Funny, when boys gather in a group their focus is on the future. "When I get older, when I get married, when I get established in my career, when I can save up enough money..."

Our present state seems too ordinary to be cherished. Ordinary day-to-day life seems too common to be appreciated. Then suddenly, when the years have passed, we look back fondly on the good old days.

After spending a season with Provo High School's basketball team, I believe a basketball season is viewed in much the same way. There is a tendency to always look ahead. They'll say, "When we play our first game. When region play starts, I can't wait for the Timpview game, or, I'm just looking forward to the state tournament."

I wonder how many players stop to enjoy the moment, to pause and ponder one thought—the way to heaven, is heaven.

I suspect most athletes will not remember many of the scores of the games they played, but I'm confident they will take away memories of a bus ride, or talking about girls with their teammates in the stands during the JV and sophomore games. They will remember the funny times during the year and relive them.

Perhaps all they will take away from their playing days is just a feeling. The feeling they had when their names were introduced in front of thousands of screaming fans. Feelings of celebrating a big win or a clutch shot. Though they may gather dust, those memories will never lose their polish.

I spent days and nights with Provo High School's basketball team with the hopes I could see how the program has become the most successful in Utah history.

I watched practices from the bench. I had shooting contests with some of the players. I went in with the team at halftime. I was in the locker room after the game. I went to dinner with the players on team nights. I was close enough to the cheers to have my ears ring, and I was within an arm's length of their disappointments.

I began to understand the highs and lows of a season as I had never experienced them before. I learned everything I always wanted to know about a basketball team, things I knew I would never have found out even if I asked.

I would like to thank coach Craig Drury and his coaching staff at Provo High for opening the bus door to their season and allowing me to come along for the ride and tell their story.

I realize it must have been a daunting and sometimes intimidating task to have someone be your shadow to the point of annoyance for four months: someone armed with a tape recorder, a pen, and a notebook, ready to write down everything that happened.

One night I asked Drury if I could come over to his home to talk basketball.

"Sure," he said. "You're welcome in my house any time." After a slight pause, he added, "At least until the book comes out."

Drury then looked at me and smiled. "No, I don't think I've done anything to embarrass myself."

Throughout the process of writing this book, I've had several people say, "You want Provo to win for your book, don't you?"

Or, "I'll bet you hope Provo wins the state championship, don't you?"

After a Provo loss I would often hear, "Too bad for your book."

Not really. The thrill of a project like this is that there is no script. Winning and losing is all impromptu. This isn't the movies. The excitement of writing about a team or someone's life is that no one knows what will happen tomorrow.

Reality TV has become so popular for just that reason—no one knows the ending. Unlike the movies, you can't change the ending just because it didn't test well with an audience.

No, what's made this book so intriguing to me is the excitement of not knowing the ending. No one knows who will win the state championship. Provo is one of several teams that, with the right breaks and bounces, could win it all.

There have been so many memorable moments that I often reflect on and smile about. There was the time when Steve Torkildson checked into the game and was quickly subbed out. He had his shorts on backwards and had a hard time keeping them from falling off.

At the next practice, the whole team showed up with their shorts on backwards.

I remember walking with assistant coach Keli Lobendahn on a Maui beach with several of the players. We were all amazed at what we missed, what we never would have seen had coach Keli not been there to show us.

I remember talking basketball with Drury for hours in his condo in Maui one night, knowing I may be the only writer to ever have such an experience.

Whenever I go to another Provo game, I will always wonder who gets the prestigious Scrub Cup, the post-game honor that is given in the locker room or on the bus to the player who made the biggest boneheaded play of the game.

And whenever I hear someone sing the national anthem off key, I'll remember the bus rides on the way home, where there were two constants: the players would sing, but their singing would always be a little out of tune.

This is the story of the 2002-03 Provo Bulldogs. It's just a peek into the lives of the coaches and players.

I've never had a more enjoyable project in the 15 years I've been a sportswriter. I was just a passenger along for the ride, but as time went on I felt like I was a kid riding on the Ferris wheel. Each time I reached the bottom, I'd look at the man running the ride. *Please don't reach for the button and stop the ride. I never want it to end. Just one more time around.*

Now the season is over. The trip is done. All that's left are photographs and memories, a few pages in the yearbook, and this. I hope you enjoy this ride as much as I did.

INTRODUCTION

Quiet! Turn off the radio. Turn on the lights, Corbin Mercer has an announcement to make.

"SCRUB CUP!" he shouts. On cue, his teammates pound on the top of the green padded seats. They play the drums on the ceiling of the bus and for a moment they are the fans.

The coaches occupy the first few seats of the bus. Next are the varsity cheerleaders, followed by the team. First the freshman and sophomores, then a mixture of juniors and seniors. The juniors and seniors always sit in the back. It's just how the pecking order has been established.

Mercer, is a 5'10" senior point guard. He is the person in charge of the team's post-game honor, the Scrub Cup.

No one on the team knows how or when the Scrub Cup tradition started. All they know is when they made the varsity team, the Scrub Cup was a tradition, and so it goes from one graduating class to another.

The Scrub Cup award is given to the player or coach who makes the dumbest or funniest play or comment of the night.

Before Mercer gets to the nominations, there is an item of business to take care of—he would like to give a shoutout to junior point guard Cory Carter. Shoutouts are part of the Scrub Cup ceremonies. It's a way of complimenting a player before they make fun of them.

Carter was the surprise star of the game. He is just 5'10" and 130 pounds, but he came off the bench to hit five three-pointers and finished with 19 points. The way Carter played, Mercer has to wonder if this is a sign of things to come. Mercer and Carter are battling for the same position—backup point guard.

"Cory, Cory, Cory," the cheerleaders chanted when he stepped onto the bus. All the practice time in the gym and the summer days when he didn't feel like getting up have just been validated.

Carter, who drained 11 three-pointers in a sophomore game last year, never received this kind of attention before. He's finding out the difference between varsity and sophomore games.

He just smiles, but that's nothing compared to what's going on inside. His heart rate is in the red. He's a little embarrassed that the spotlight has settled on his seat in the bus after the game, but it sure feels good.

Now it's time for tonight's nominations.

Tika (Tee-Ka) Wesley, the team's 6'5", 230 pound senior center, is the first nomination. He is the team's inside threat. He is powerful inside the key and knows how to use his weight to create some space to get an open shot, but sometimes his physical play can draw offensive fouls. Tonight, he was saddled with three quick fouls and played less than two quarters the entire game.

This is a weak nomination, but it's the first game of a new season, and the team is still trying to find its niche.

Other nominations are announced: head coach Craig Drury, who jumped up and did a 360 spin after Carter hit his fourth three-pointer of the night. This is a legitimate nomination, but no one really wants to give their coach the first Scrub Cup of the season, so other nominations are announced.

Joe Pututau (Poo-too-t-ow), a 6'3" senior shooting guard, was 0 for 7 for the night from the field.

Mick Hagen, a 6'0" senior point guard, had his shot blocked by a 6'8" reserve player late in the game.

Nominations are now closed. No voting is done. The decision for the first Scrub Cup rests with Mercer and no one else.

That's not to say Mercer can't be influenced. Scrub Cup bribery is not only legal, but it's encouraged. Mercer is open to comments from his teammates.

After careful consideration, Provo's first Scrub Cup of the 2002-03 season goes to Tika Wesley.

Mercer hands Wesley a flattened Taco Bell cup that he dug out of a garbage can. This is also a tradition. The Scrub Cup winner never gets anything that you'd want to put on your mantle. It's always a used cup.

Cory Carter dribbles by a Pleasant Grove defender. Carter surprised everyone when he hit five 3-pointers and opened the season with 19 points.

"Speech, speech!" This is a requirement.

"What can I say? I'm honored to win the first Scrub Cup. At least I didn't play long enough to do something stupid."

There is a Scrub Cup tonight because the team opened the 2002-03 season with a 56-47 win at Copper Hills.

If the team loses, the Scrub Cup ceremony is skipped. No one wants to laugh at themselves or their teammates after a loss.

The win was no surprise. Provo comes into the season ranked No. 2 in division 4A. There are five classifications in Utah High School athletics.

What's the difference between 5A and 1A?

Enrollment. Numbers. Travel. Athletes.

Alta High School, located in Sandy, Utah, is 20 miles south of Salt Lake City and is the largest school in the state with an enrollment of 2,461. The smallest is Elk Dale near the Nevada border with an enrollment of just 18.

Copper Hills is 5A, with an enrollment of 1,776. Provo is 4A with an enrollment of 1,240 (10-12th grades).

There are over 10,000 high schools in Texas. In Utah there are 124 that are part of the High School Activities Association, but when it comes to producing professional athletes, Utah holds its own.

In football, some of the biggest names are: Chad Lewis, a Pro Bowl tight end with the Philadelphia Eagles; Kevin Dyson, a wide receiver with the Carolina Panthers; and Doug Jolley, a tight end with the Oakland Raiders.

In basketball, there's Shawn Bradley with the Dallas Mavericks; Travis Knight with the New York Knicks; Britton Johnson with the Orlando Magic; and Travis Hansen with the Atlanta Hawks. Fred Roberts and several other players have had brief NBA careers—guys like Jeff Judkins, Josh Grant, Devin Durrant, and Bret Vroman have also played in the NBA.

For the last two years, Utah's Ragu Classic has brought in some of the top teams from around the country. There have been 15 different Utah teams to participate in the tournament. Utah's record against some of the nation's top schools is 10-13.

The best team in Utah varies from year to year, but there's one constant when talking about high school basketball in Utah:

Provo High School is always near the top.

No school has won more often than Provo. The Bulldogs hold the state record of 14 state championships. The next closest school is Lehi (3A) with 11 titles. Jordan (5A) and South Sevier (2A) are next with eight each.

So it's no surprise that the Bulldogs have opened the season with a win. Copper Hills won the 5A title in 2000, but since then haven't been able to recapture the magic and have been middle of the pack of 5A schools.

The win over Copper Hills was nothing for the coaching staff to celebrate. Their assessment of the game was that the team played below par, and that's only a compliment in golf.

The offense was sluggish, and the defense had too many lapses. But even a bad win is much better than a loss, so they're content with knowing the learning curve can still be accomplished without a blemish on their record.

After the game the players don't think much of improvement or what they could do differently. Other things occupy their thoughts, particularly because there are cheerleaders are on the bus.

It's now time for another tradition. Singing. No nickel needed. The acappella jukebox plays after every win. There's no volume control. No input on the selections. You take what you get.

Tonight's selections are "I'll Make Love to You," by Boyz II Men, an odd choice, but it's followed by a more appropriate selection, "I Feel Wonderful Tonight," by Eric Clapton.

For some reason, those two songs are the only ones each of the players know word for word.

Steve Torkildson, a 6'6" reserve forward, has recently followed the pom-poms of a blonde cheerleader named Jackie, who is sitting near the front of the bus. They have been dating for just two weeks.

Arrangements are made. He gets another cheerleader named Tara to move up a seat so he can sneak up to sit by Jackie: a violation of bus etiquette—no sitting by the cheerleaders, no funny stuff—but the two get away with it for about five minutes before the coaches look back and spot them. Torkildson gets up and goes back to his own seat.

It's a good thing the team won, or the coaches might not have been so willing to forget about it.

The bus pulls back up to the school 35 minutes after it pulled out of the Copper Hills parking lot.

The first night of the 2002-03 season is over. The team is embarking on a season of incredible highs and lows, laugher and tears. It's one they will never forget.

Pututau walks off the bus trying to forget about his 0-7 night. Whew! At least he didn't get the Scrub Cup.

He has no idea how differently he will feel in another week.

CHAPTER ONE

THE NIGHT THE DREAM CAME TRUE

Despite a foot of snow piled up around an icy driveway, the faint sound of a basketball can be heard echoing around the neighborhood.

Passing cars slow down to stare. What is that kid doing outside shooting hoops at 9 p.m. in the middle of January? They don't understand this is where dreams live. This is where the countdown begins.

The play is called.

10-9-8.

You dribble behind your back.

7-6-5-4.

You make a spin move around two would-be defenders.

3-2-1.

You pull up for the game-winning shot.

Buzz!

It's good! Unbelievable. What a shot! It's good!

The crowd spills onto the court like a two-litter bottle of A&W that's been stuck on a paint-mixing machine. You're mobbed. Your teammates hug you, the cheerleaders kiss you.

You're carried off the court a hero. But when the fans finally lower you down from their shoulders, you realize the crowd consists of just one person. The screams and cheers are made up of just one voice—yours.

You are the only one cheering, despite your best efforts to imitate the echo of cheers by putting your hand over your mouth and quickly taking it away over and over again.

Then you take the ball inbounds where the countdown begins again.

3-2-1 . . .

Buzz!

It's no good. But wait. A foul was called. You couldn't hear the whistle in the pandemonium.

Free throws to win the game.

Swish, swish. Unbelievable. Mr. Clutch. With 15,000 fans watching and the bright light of the TV cameras on, you hit two of the biggest free throws of your life.

All around the country, from a playground in Lahainaluna, Maui, to the outdoor courts down the street, the dream for basketball players is the same—to hit a game-winning shot at the buzzer.

For some that dream comes true; for most, it only lives on in their driveways.

Joey Pututau is one of the lucky ones. He has lived that dream.

At first glance, it's hard to find any blemishes in Pututau's life. He's a good student. He carried a 3.57 GPA into his senior year. He fits the stereotype: he's tall, dark, and handsome. He has dark skin—the combination of a white mother and a Tongan father. His teeth never needed to be whitened. He's not obnoxiously loud. In fact, he's more reserved and on the quiet, humble side. He has a girlfriend, Julie, that his friends call "The wife," even though they have only dated four months. Fearing they would get too serious, her parents required she go to one of the school dances with someone else at least once.

Most high school students get into some kind of trouble during their time of walking the high school halls, but the most mischief Pututau gets into is trying to con a Pizza Hut employee into giving him a free pizza.

When the team went to a tournament in Hawaii, he went out with teammates Mick Hagen and Scott Ady. It was getting dark and Pututau was still wearing his sunglasses.

Others looked at him strangely, thinking he was blind, which gave the three an idea. Why not pretend he was blind? So, Ady and Hagen led Pututau into Pizza Hut where they tried to play on the sympathy of one the employees.

"Can I help you?" asked the man behind the counter.

Hagen pulled out two dollars from his pocket and said to Pututau,

Joey Pututau reaches for a rebound in a game against Lehi. Pututau once scored 51 points in a summer league game, but that was nothing compared to the two points he scored at the buzzer against Mountain View.

"I only have two dollars."

There was a pause, hoping the Pizza Hut employee would offer up a freebee.

But the employee wasn't taking the bait. It would require a better sales job.

Pututau finally responded. "I think I have some money in my pocket. I have a $10 and a $5."

He pulled out two bills, but they were both one dollar bills. What a move. What a nice touch. The act appeared to be working.

Another long pause.

"I'm really hungry," Pututau added.

Another pause doesn't work. Still unmoved by their plight, the scrooge behind the counter just waits for their order.

It's then that they realize their error. They have four dollars, which is actually enough to buy a small pizza.

Looking back on it, Pututau realized his mistake. "We should have come in with just two dollars," he said with laugh.

But all was not lost. The free pizza con isn't going to work, but he sure would like a drink.

"I'm so thirsty. I wish I could have a big old drink," Pututau says as he turns in a direction where no one is standing, hoping to play one more sympathy card.

Bingo!

The employee hands Hagen a large drink cup. The three leave with a small pizza, a free drink, and a good laugh.

For Pututau, that's as much trouble as he gets into, and considering his situation, that may be a small miracle.

Pututau's father married his mother Rochelle. The couple had Tony three years before they had Joey.

Two years later the Pututau family was severed. The couple divorced and the Pututau boys have been primarily raised by their mother ever since.

When asked if Joey is a momma's boy, Rochelle replies, "He doesn't have a choice."

Even though Joey's father lives in Provo, he rarely comes to a game and isn't an active part of his life.

"The kid has never given me any kind of grief. I don't know

where he came from," Rochelle says. "He's very directed. I don't know how. He never sees his dad."

Instead, Pututau's mother has become the center of his life.

Every Sunday, she cooks up his favorite meal—chicken fried steak and mashed potatoes.

A game isn't a game without mom there to watch. Whenever he plays, he always looks to the stands for his mom. When eye contact is made, he can relax.

When Pututau was a freshman, he played baseball. Rochelle dropped him off for the game 30 minutes early and went to run some errands.

When she came back the game was in the third inning. The other parents filled her in on what happened.

"There you are," one parent said. Joey keeps asking where you went, when you'll be back."

When Joey was in the fifth grade, he was named class president, but deferred the honor. He told his teacher, "Why don't you give it to Adam? I think he needs it more than I do."

He is a member of the school's chess club and is involved in crime prevention. Both activities can be traced to Hagen's influence. The two found out the Crime Prevention Club had a trip planned to Florida, so they signed up.

"Some of the thugs at school call me 'Narc-cop' and 'goodie, goodie,' but overall, they're still good to me," Joey says in a tone that makes you wonder if anyone dislikes this guy.

He's an Eagle Scout and for his Eagle project, he gathered clothing and books to send to the poor in the Philippines. Included in the shipment to the Philippines was Pututau's favorite book.

"The book was called *The Danger Zone*. I read it three times. It's about a player who gets into a zone and wins the game at the buzzer," Pututau says.

An omen.

Despite his other interests that include tennis, golf, fishing and girls, he's settled on one sport to excel at—hoops.

As a junior he played only a few minutes a game, but now as a senior, he's the team's shooting guard and the player the team counts on to score consistently.

In a summer league game he scored 51 points. In practice he admits to making 27 three-pointers in a row one time.

He's arguably the team's best outside shooter. Over the years since he started playing organized basketball in the third grade, just how many times has he ever sunk the game-winning shot?

Two? Three? Four?

Never.

But on Friday, December 6, 2002, Pututau's dream came true.

Provo hosted the Mountain View Bruins, a team that former coach Rob Cuff had turned into a powerhouse. Under Cuff's seven years as head coach at Mountain View, he won two state championships and made the semifinals four times. He made sure the team never finished lower than fifth.

Even though both schools are 4A, they play in different regions (divisions). Mountain View (Region 7) has turned into one of Provo's (Region 6) bigger rivals in basketball and has played against Provo as well as anyone, including Timpview.

In 22 years of playing against Provo, Mountain View had a 15-17 record.

But Cuff left in 2001, taking a job with the Utah High School Activities Association. Mountain View hired Jason Young, the head coach at Morgan High School, to take over.

In Young's first year, the Bruins won a Region 7 title, but struggled to reach their potential and finished with a 12-10 record.

After the season, Young watched five players transfer to other schools.

So Provo figured there was no one left at Mountain View. This would be an easy game.

Funny how the minds of teenage athletes work.

This year's batch of Bruins didn't figure to be able to hang with Provo, but to everyone's surprise, Mountain View stunned the Bulldogs in the first half. The vaunted Provo defense had been shredded by a bunch of no-names.

The Bruins torched the Bulldogs for 19 first-quarter points and took a 19-13 lead at the end of the first quarter. Mountain View continued to control the game, scoring the final four points of the half to take a 31-22 lead into the locker room.

It's obvious to Provo's coaches that the team members are playing like they thought this game would be easy.

It's time to light a fire.

Assistant coach Jeff Schoonover has evidence to Provo's meltdown. "We've had 12 turnovers and just five assists. They're having way too much fun on our court."

Coach Drury doesn't yell or scream, but his voice is firm and direct. It's clear that adrenaline is pumping through his veins.

"Personnel changes, that's what we need."

He then turns his attention to Hagen, the team's point guard and the player that runs the team's offense. Hagen's first name is Michael, but almost everyone calls him Mick, except Drury.

"Mike, I don't think you want to play basketball this year," Drury says as he talks about Hagen's defense on transition and a turnover where he threw a pass right to a Bruin defender.

Assistant coach Keli Lobendahn chips in. "Have you ever seen wild dogs defending a kill? They foam at the mouth. They'll do anything to defend their kill. I don't see any foaming at the mouth."

Provo storms out of the locker room. Forward Tai Wesley immediately pulls down an offensive rebound and scores. Forward Craig Stringham blocks a shot from Mountain View's Nate Allman. Hagen then feeds center Tika Wesley with an assist that leads to an easy hoop.

The Provo comeback continues through the third quarter, and after baskets from forward Craig Stringham and Tika, the quarter ends with Mountain View's lead down to one at 39-38.

Neither team can open up a big lead in the fourth quarter as the game comes down to the final seconds. The Bruins lead 54-49 with a minute left. It looks like Mountain View will pull off the upset.

But Hagen whips the ball to Pututau on the wing and he buries a three-pointer. Pututau then comes up with a steal and gives it up to Hagen, who passes it inside to Tika, who scores and is fouled.

Provo now has a chance to take the lead, but Tika misses the free throw and Mountain View gets the rebound and calls a timeout.

The Bruins draw up a play for the win, but they miss the shot, and Provo pulls down the rebound with five seconds left in the game.

Now it's Drury who calls a timeout and draws up a play.

The plan was to have Pututau inbound the ball. He would get it to Cory Carter, who would look to Pututau first in the corner. If he was covered, Carter would try plan B.

No need.

Pututau was left open in the corner.

The clock ticked down. Four, three, two.

Pututau spots up a foot behind the three-point line and shoots.

Swish!

Buzz! It's good! Provo wins 57-54.

Fans pour onto the court. Hagen hugs Pututau and lifts him into the air. Pututau smiles a smile that has never been captured on film.

How sweet it is. The celebration continued all night. Pututau was joined by Hagen and Ady. They went to eat at Subway, then to the stomp, a victory dance.

At the stomp, he didn't need to relive the shot, everyone else would do that for him.

"As soon as you got the ball, I started running toward the court, I knew it was going in."

"Great shot!"

"Way to come up clutch."

"Pututau is money."

Provo's PA announcer Saia Pope is also an assistant football coach at Provo and is an aspiring rapper.

Pope decided to do an impromptu; he would rap on the spot, and include Pututau and Tika Wesley.

What a night. Pututau danced with "the wife" mostly and occasionally ventured out to dance with some other girls. It was a yearbook moment. If there was ever a lesson on seizing the day and enjoying the journey, this was it.

Provo didn't play another game for a week. The team's next game was at home against Lone Peak.

Before the Lone Peak game, Pututau sat in the stands and waited for the JV game to end. When asked if the thrill had worn off yet, Pututau said, "What?" with an obvious smile.

His week of celebration was over. The next game against Lone Peak was just minutes away.

The game of basketball has a short memory. It never cares what you did a day ago, a week ago, a career ago. Every game is a new chapter.

Provo turned in an impressive 57-42 win over Lone Peak. The combination of center Tika Wesley (24 points) and forward Tai Wesley (15 points), along with 10 points from Hagen proved to be too much for the Knights.

As for Pututau, he didn't score.

CHAPTER 2

THE PUZZLE THAT IS MICK HAGEN

One light flickers inside the Hagen house. The rest of the house has been put to bed hours ago, but in the study, the glow from a computer screen shines, and on the desk a single lightbulb shines just bright enough to let Mick Hagen see what he's doing.

It's 4 a.m., and his alarm clock is set to go off in two hours for another school day. But sleep can wait. It usually does. Hagen has work to do.

Name: Michael Hagen

City: Provo, Utah

Race: Hispanic

Interests: There's not enough room in the box

Hagen is putting the finishing touches on his state Sterling Scholar application for Computer Science.

He continues with the application.

Computer Background: Winner of Computer Technology Sterling Scholar Award for Provo High School. He is the school webmaster and has created Web sites for the National Honor Society, the Science Club, and the Youth Crime Watch. He is the President and Founder of the Provo High School Computer Club.

GPA: 3.99

ACT Score: 29

Qualifications: One of just 10 players in the 4A classification to be named Academic All-State.

Project: Currently creating a new Web site called **dawgma.com**, where Provo High School students can type in the address and in minutes find out how other students feel about school, the faculty, college, and their future.

If you want to make Mick Hagen break out in uncontrollable bouts of laughter, call him a dumb jock.

Nothing could more ridiculous.

Truth is, no one really knows what to call Mick Hagen. Labels don't fit. It's kind of like describing Tracy Chapman's music. Is it country? Pop? Folk? Rock?

Actually, it's none of them. Her music is unique unto itself.

Like Mick Hagen?

Exactly.

As the Editor in Chief of *The Provoian*, the high school newspaper, it seemed only fitting that since no one else has been able to describe Hagen, that he do it himself.

When asked to write a paragraph to describe himself, this is what he wrote.

> *Gypsies, princes, and kings from all over the world came to see this puzzle. All came in hopes of solving it, but the puzzle of Mick Hagen was too difficult.*
>
> *Their efforts were in vain.*
>
> *No one can put me together. And I don't know if anyone ever will. I have innumerable pieces. They are all shaped differently, colored differently, and sized differently. They lay scattered across my floor waiting patiently for some extraordinary event. Many confident problem solvers take one glance at my puzzle and quickly run the other way. Other people will stay long enough to look into my eyes, but depart daunted by the mystery and obscurity which I hold.*
>
> *Some people get close to solving this puzzle, but soon realize more pieces are added, some pieces are taken away and some pieces are transformed.*
>
> *Oedipus once tried solving me. He couldn't do it.*
>
> *I am unique. I am weird. People have no idea where to begin when trying to solve me. My oddness goes far beyond my minor obsessions for showering in the dark, putting my right sock on before my left, or eating a slice of pizza starting with the crust.*
>
> *I baffle; I bewilder; Yet, I enlighten; I inspire.*
>
> *I am a nerd. I am a Hispanic. I am a jock. I am a leader.*
>
> *Solve me, scatter me, box me or bag me. I am a puzzle.*
>
> *I am Mick Hagen.*

This is the leader of Provo High School's basketball team. The chances of the team winning a record 15th state tournament title rest largely on his shoulders.

He is the point guard. The team feeds off his energy. The offense runs through his hands. As far as talent goes, few could disagree that he's the most talented player on the team. He is arguably the best shooter on the team. He is the best ball-handler and best free-throw shooter. He is a seasoned veteran when it comes to high school basketball.

Hagen has been starting since he was a sophomore, a rare feat at Provo. Now as a senior, those looking at Provo High School as a title contender will have to look Hagen squarely in the eyes to gauge Provo's chances.

He has the talent to be a superstar at 6'1" and 175, to play at virtually any Division I school in the country, if only he would concentrate on basketball. Eat, drink, and breathe the game. Live it.

But he can't. He won't. There are too many other interests in life. Basketball is a priority, but it's not his only priority. The pie is cut into too many pieces.

Drury has one problem with Hagen—commitment. In Drury's view, Mick's off-court interests in other things are hurting his game on the court and hurting the team.

Mick admits if he lifted weights more in the summer and spent more time perfecting his game, he would be a better basketball player, but his reasoning is logical, just like one of his chess moves.

"God gave me a talent to play basketball, which I have worked to develop," he says. "But he also gave me other talents. Why shouldn't I develop those?"

No one will accuse Michael Hagen of neglecting to develop other talents. After he visited Taiwan, he thought the language was cool, so just for kicks he decided to take a class in Chinese at Brigham Young University.

While in Taiwan he also pursued another interest—photography. He snapped a series of pictures of the locals, including several shots of children that look like they came from the pages of *Life Magazine*.

Instead, his photo was published in "Images of the Mind," an anthology created by the International Library of Photography after

Mick Hagen (left) talks to teammate Joey Pututau during a game. Hagen and Pututau have been best friends since the 6th grade.

he was a semifinalist in the International Open Amateur Photographer Contest.

He had also hoped to audition for a part in the school's production of *West Side Story*, but tryouts clashed with basketball, so he decided to concentrate on the state tournament.

Hagen is clearly no ordinary jock, but has all the benefits of being one. He likes to dance and has no trouble getting asked by a variety of different girls. He goes on more dates than anyone on the team, but he's picky—very picky. He's also very smooth and has no trouble finding a different girl to date each week.

It's not uncommon for girls from the other schools Provo plays to ask Hagen to pose for a picture with them or for the girls to give him their phone numbers.

As the season goes on he would meet a girl from nearly every school the team played. After a game at Orem High School, Hagen met a student from Orem. She gave him her number, and they talked for several hours that night and within a week he was dating her.

When Provo played at Spanish Fork, he ran into a female student he went out with once who was shooting photos for the Spanish Fork yearbook.

"See if you can get some good shots of me and then email them to me okay?" Mick said. He then followed up with, "We went out once," explaining their relationship.

"We never really did a real date," she responded.

"Yeah, well, invite me to one of your dances. Call me. I would go with you if you ever need a date," Hagen continued.

"Yeah, we need to have a real date," the girl said.

There were several other possibilities. A section of Spanish Fork girls showed up at the game with a variety of signs aimed at distracting Provo.

One said, "No. 11 (Hagen's number), you're my dream boat."

After the game was over, with some encouragement, he took off his white head band and threw it to the group of girls with the signs. They scrambled for the head band as if it was the bouquet from a wedding.

Hagen's charm apparently crosses all age barriers. After one game, he was asked to come out of the locker room to talk to a five-year old girl, who thought he was cute and wanted to meet him.

Still, this bachelor is tired of playing the field.

In one of his weekly columns in the school newspaper—a column he calls, "Mick's Musings,"—the headline reads, "I'm still searching."

Hagen's column gives him a chance to talk about one of his favorite subjects—women.

> *"Yes, it's true. I am indeed, a zany, pocket-protected, perm-infested geek whose one wish is simple, yet daunting."*
>
> *"Santa Claus, I want a girlfriend. It is fun to live on a leash sometimes...I must admit."*

He continues.

> *"I'm jealous of some of my best friends. They have girlfriends, life just isn't fair. They may live in bondage, but they are happy. They are secure, and they are very satisfied . . . in more ways than one."*

Hagen ends with, *"I want a girlfriend and I want one now."*

In anticipation of getting a response, there is a place for applications to be accepted by email.

Hagen said the column was done in jest. It was a joke. But he still got four or five applications. Hagen has no trouble attracting girls, he just can't find one he likes well enough to keep dating her. So in an effort to help, Pututau and teammate Scott Ady set a deadline for Hagen to find a girlfriend. The first day of February. No exceptions.

Now they're taking bets on whether or not Hagen will meet the deadline.

But girls aren't the distraction the coaches worry about with Hagen; it's everything else. He often bears the brunt of the criticism when the team isn't playing well.

Drury never yells at Hagen. He's found that Mick doesn't respond to that, but he is firm and often direct in his disappointment if he feels like Hagen isn't playing up to his potential. He knows there's gold buried under the surface and he's constantly searching for a way to mine it out of him.

Perhaps the reason why Drury is harder on Hagen than most is because he knows Hagen has something special, which was evident at an early age.

Hagen had just turned nine years old when he and his brothers were booked to perform at halftime of the European World Basketball Championships.

The year is 1993 and the place is Olympic Halle in Munich, Germany. The German national team has surprised many and made it to the finals against Russia. The game is being played on the same court where Russia beat the USA for the gold medal in the 1972 Olympics, one of the most controversial games in Olympic history. The USA team chose not to accept their silver medals.

It's on this same court in Germany where the Hagen brothers, known as the Whiz Kids, are providing the halftime entertainment.

Mick's oldest brother is introduced first. Blake "Ice Man" Hagen, followed by Brad "Maverick" Hagen. The brothers take their nicknames from the movie *Top Gun*. Now it's Mick's turn. Mike "Goose" Hagen, who is just eight at the time, and finally his younger brother, the scene stealer, Jeff "Hollywood" Hagen.

"Welcome the Whiz Kids from Rockville, Maryland." They take the court in front of 10,000 screaming fans.

The Whiz Kids have plenty of volunteers for their show. They take turns dribbling three and four balls at a time. They spin basketballs on the tip of a spoon, then feed the volunteer pudding while the ball continues to spin on the spoon.

Mick puts on a three-point shooting display, and little Jeff does dribbling tricks and shoots from around the court.

After the show is over, fans mob the brothers as if they were rock stars or royalty. They want autographs and pictures. They just want to touch them and are willing to push and shove the person next to them to get what they want.

Jeff has just learned to write his name, but it takes him too long to sign it, so he usually just signs a "J" on whatever is put in front of him.

Who would have thought it would have come to this? It started by accident. Mick's father Dave bought a basketball "How To" video by NBA legend "Pistol" Pete Maravich.

The results were predictable. Within days, all four boys were trying to spin the ball on their fingers, working on behind-the-back passes, and inventing new ways to dribble the ball.

Their skills were noticed at a basketball camp and word soon spread. The boys were invited to entertain at a children's hospital where a writer from the Washington Post fell in love with their act.

They were featured on the front page of the Metro section of the *Washington Post* and within hours after the article hit the streets, the Hagen family's world changed.

The show *Good Morning America* sent their limo to pick them up and bring them to the studio to perform on the show. *Sports Illustrated for Kids* did a spread on the Whiz Kids, and they started doing halftime shows at college and NBA games.

Blake and Brad anchored the show with ball-handling tricks and spinning basketballs on such things as pens and the corners of books. Mick shot three-pointers from NBA range, and Jeff "Hollywood" Hagen was just so cute he could do no wrong. At just four years old, he shot from areas inside the key. With every shot he made, the crowd went crazy.

"It was great because we got to see the world, and we did it on their dime," Dave Hagen said. "Every city we'd go to we always made sure we went to a museum or a historical place. We wanted it to be an educational experience as well."

One stop in particular impressed Mick.

It was at a college campus.

"I told him this is where the best go. If you want to compete with the best, this is where you do it," Dave recalls.

Mick gazed around at the surroundings. This was awesome. Some day he would be back. The place?

Harvard.

The Hagens have videos of their stops around the country. The most memorable was at Boston Garden, where the boys hardly missed a shot.

Hollywood, i.e. Jeff, couldn't miss. He made seven straight shots inside the key. The crowd went crazy. Mick made an attempt at dribbling four balls at once. Even though he couldn't keep them going for long, Celtic fans sensed this was better than what they'd paid to see.

Mick then hit a long NBA three-pointer, then turned around and raised his arms like he had just tamed a lion. The crowd ate it up. They were putty in his hands.

"I had a lot of coaches who would come up to me and point to Mick and say, 'That one is your player. He's going to be a great one,'" Dave said. "We kind of knew all along that he was the most talented of the group."

Dave grew up in Maryland and after a few years of college at BYU returned home to Maryland where he got into real estate and met his wife Annabella, who had moved to Maryland from Guatemala when she was 17. The two were married and stayed in Maryland until they thought it would be best to move to Utah.

In 1992 the Hagens moved to Utah. Annabella, a respected child therapist, received her master's degree in social work. Dave now runs his own business.

By 1996 the brothers were getting older and their interests were changing. The Whiz Kids act was getting old, literally, so Dave pulled the plug on the tour, but not before the family had stockpiled a lifetime of memories and memorabilia.

There's a room in the Hagen house that features a variety of memories, including jerseys from the Russian and German teams that they had performed for in the World Championships.

There's a Harlem Globetrotter autographed ball. There's an autographed ball from the Chicago Bulls' 1991 season that includes Michael Jordan. On the wall there's autographed jerseys from Alonzo Mourning and Larry Bird. There's another jersey signed by Shaquille O'Neal when he was with the Orlando Magic.

Those were the days, but times have changed.

Brad, the oldest, started for Provo as a junior. He had a solid but unspectacular career. Blake tried out for the team but got cut. Jeff, the star of the Whiz Kids, is a sophomore, but he tells his father he no longer wants to play basketball. He wants to turn his attention to tennis.

Mick is a different story. He started as a sophomore and as a junior, he averaged 10 points and 4 assists. Now as a senior he is expecting to have a breakout season.

He sometimes still gets called "Whiz Kid" by opposing fans who try to taunt him. Even his teammates will play the Whiz Kid trump card once in a while.

So the pressure of winning rides on Hagen's shoulders like he just strapped on a pair of shoulder pads, and maybe it's fitting that it worked out that way.

Hagen is a nerd. He's a jock. He's a leader. No one is sure just what to call Mick Hagen, just as no one is sure how the season will turn out. Will he lead the team to a title? Will he harness the greatness within?

Over the years Hagen has played in Provo's program, Drury has figured out that Hagen is a complex puzzle—much like that of a high school basketball season.

Now he must figure out how to solve this puzzle, because he is Provo's best hope in its quest to obtain another green banner.

CHAPTER THREE

COACH

On a typical night during the season, Craig Drury can be found downstairs in his basement. He's not drawing up new plays or watching film on another team. He's not in the middle of a coaches meeting or thumbing through photos albums reliving championships of the past.

On this night, Drury is helping his youngest daughter Hollie work on a science project. He's busy cutting out pieces of wood to make a frame for the blue board that will be used as the display.

It's not long before one of Drury's other daughters, Cassie, comes downstairs to show her father the engagement ring she just received. She holds out her hand for approval.

"That's beautiful," Dad says.

Cassie gives her father a smile, the kind that only comes from the excitement of being engaged.

These girls love their dad. Not one or two of them, but all seven of Drury's daughters. In a twist of irony, Drury—the man who bleeds green, the coach who has 362 career wins, the guy who has five state championships (the most of any active coach in Utah)—has seven girls. Four of them were cheerleaders, a few played basketball, but none of them played past their junior year. Oh well, surely Drury would have a son who played.

Nope, he and his wife Robin never had a boy.

Drury is surrounded by women, there is no escaping that fact. Naturally, he has thought about what it would have been like to coach his son, but he no longer wrestles with that "What if" scenario.

"I think God was merciful to me. He knew if I had a son, I probably would have been brutal on him," Drury said. "You hear stories about a kid who misses free throws at Junior Jazz games and his father, who is the coach, has him down at the gym until midnight shooting free throws. I hope I wouldn't be that bad, but if he wanted to play, I'd want him to play hard and maybe my son would not play that way."

The father/son relationship is difficult enough, but when you add a coach/player label to the relationship, it only complicates the matter.

Drury recalls a story that former Provo coach Jim Spencer told him when Spencer had a son play for him.

"They agreed to only talk basketball during practice. They got in the car one night after practice to drive home, and the first thing he (Spencer) said was, 'You've got to work on your rebounding.'"

So who is this man of many daughters and why has he won so often? How has he helped maintain the basketball tradition at Provo High School in a day when the competitive advantage is gone and there's more parity in the league than ever before?

Coaches are waiting with pen and paper in hand. They are ready to photocopy his blueprint and have him teach them the secret to his success. The problem is, it's a complicated equation. He is a man of many dimensions, and he is constantly balancing priorities of family, school and coaching.

But here's a peek into his play book. Here's a look inside his office. If you want to know what fuels his fire, let's start with the basics. Let's climb inside his head and delve into his past.

Where to start? Let's start by going inside his heart. If he were giving a speech for "Coach of the Year," he would surely thank his wife, Robin, and his family.

Behind every good coach is either a good wife or a divorce certificate. No one coaches for 27 years without one or the other.

On behalf of the thousands of coaches' wives around the country, Robin Drury would like to say something: "Sometimes I feel like he's married to basketball."

For all the young coaches around the country, for all the wives of coaches, guess what? For many it never changes. It never does get better. Get used to it.

From November to the first week in March, Robin is a basketball widow—even after 31 years of marriage.

If you have ever picked up a magazine and read the top 10 reasons for divorce, then you know there are the usual problems. Stuff like financial problems, infidelity, work-a-holics, lack of similar interests.

What should have made the list was marrying a high school basketball coach. Think about it. Years of devotion away from home and all for what? Financial security?

Please.

Think of it this way. Who would answer this ad?

> **Help Wanted:** Seasonal position, 11 months out of the year. Must have exceptional knowledge of basketball and be willing to scout and fundraise. Must be willing to work nights and weekends, including summers. Must be willing to handle parent complaints from those seeking to get you fired and supervise up to 25 kids, between the ages of 14-18. Pay is $1.50 an hour.

The pay is not an exaggeration. Drury, in his 20th year as head coach, will make an estimated $3,000 this season. When you add up practice time, game preparation, scouting, summer leagues, open gym, tournaments, and fundraising, Drury figures he'll work over 1,500 hours during the year.

Why would anyone do it for one year, much less for 20 years?

For the love of the game.

"I never got a master's degree, mainly because I don't have time," Drury said. "That may sound like a cop-out, but I've spent so much time in the summer, because I want to help them be better players if possible."

Not all wives would be so patient, a fact that Drury readily acknowledges. Not all wives would work for 15 years so he could pursue his dream to coach. He knows he's a lucky man. He has someone to go home to and talk with about the game.

"There's some games when he wins and it's like he lost," Robin says.

The life of a coach's wife.

Even though Drury doesn't pull in a six-figure income, he hit the lottery at age 14.

"We met when we were 14 at a BYU football game," he said. "She went to a different junior high, but some of her friends knew me, and when she looked through the yearbook, she pointed at my picture and said, 'That's going to be my boyfriend.'"

Robin Drury was right. When they got to high school, they dated on a regular basis. Both went out with other people, but they never went very long without seeing each other.

As a sophomore in high school, Drury was a three-sport star. His players may snicker at the thought of Drury dunking the ball now that his hair has turned gray and he often wears glasses around his neck when he needs to read something. Just because most of the excess weight he's accumulated over the years has ended up around his waist doesn't mean he wasn't one of the top players in the state in his day.

In basketball Drury led Provo in scoring and rebounding as a sophomore. He also started in football and baseball as a sophomore. How many people can say that?

Mike Gardner, former Davis High School coach, remembers Drury when Gardner was coaching at Spanish Fork. "He was a very strong, physical player in high school. He was sure a competitor. He just always played so hard."

Drury has channeled the same competitiveness he harnessed as a player into coaching. It's harder for Jim Carrey to lie in the movie *Liar, Liar* than it is for Drury to say the word "lose."

Former provo coach Dolan Condie was the coach during Drury's his sophomore and junior years. He retired at the end of Drury's junior season.

"He was a very talented individual," Condie said of Drury "He had a great jump shot and drove to the basket very well. I considered him an all-state player."

Provo was so dominating that Drury played a big role in Provo's streak of 47 straight wins in league play.

Jim Spencer succeeded Condie as coach, but Spencer never got to see Drury at his best. Midway through his senior season, after Provo's rival game against Orem, Drury broke his wrist and missed the rest of the season.

Drury played for the state championship three times but took second every time—twice in baseball and once in football. He never got to the championship as a basketball player. He graduated from Provo High in 1970 and didn't have to look far to find a place to play. He was recruited by former BYU coach Stan Watts.

As a freshman, Drury played on BYU's freshman team (freshman were not allowed to play on the varsity team) where he averaged 15 points per game and played every game except one. But Watts was diagnosed with cancer during the season, and at the end of the year Drury sat down with one of Watts' assistants and got the impression he wasn't wanted.

"My neighbor's son was an assistant coach at Southern Colorado (Pueblo)," Drury said. "They offered me a scholarship and planned to redshirt me that year."

So Drury was off to Colorado, but he first had some business to take care of. He didn't want to go to Colorado alone, so he asked Robin to marry him in August before he left.

She said yes and Drury's life changed. The Drurys went to Pueblo, but they didn't stay long. The couple returned at the Thanksgiving break, and while they were home Drury called Watts to see how he was doing.

Watts had returned to his position as head coach and asked Drury where he went. Drury told him that he didn't think he was wanted. Watts assured him he was wanted, so Drury returned to BYU and redshirted at BYU for the rest of the season.

But once again, Drury's college career took a twist. Watts resigned at the end of the year when his cancer worsened, and BYU hired Glenn Potter as his repacement. As is often the case when a new coach takes over, there are changes. Potter thought he could find better players than Drury, so Drury's second trip to BYU turned out to be his last.

Drury had other options. He had several other schools interested in him, but Robin was now pregnant so he decided to give up basketball and get through school.

"I'm not saying I would have been something special, but I do think I would have been a four-year player. I was a 6'2", slow white guy who had a decent shot and could drive to the basket well," Drury explained. "I don't have any bitterness for Potter. He's a good man. I don't think he was a great judge of talent. He had walk-ons that were beating out the kids he brought in."

Drury was right. Potter compiled a 42-36 record at BYU in his three years as head coach.

Drury moved on without basketball. In 1976 he graduated from BYU with a degree in P.E. and a minor in history.

Drury had already mapped out his future, and it didn't include coaching. He had been working construction with his cousin while he was in college. The two formed a bond and were good at what they did. Business was good, the money was good, and besides, he was a pretty darn good official. He had his eye on working his way up the ladder of officiating. Coaching and teaching weren't much of a consideration.

He did have a degree, though, and wound up with three opportunities. One was at Bountiful High School, just north of Salt Lake City, one at a small school in southern Utah, and one with a school in California. Drury wanted to be head coach at small school or junior varsity coach at bigger school, and Bountiful had an opening for the JV job. He took it.

But in two years as an assistant coach at Bountiful, the varsity team won just two games per season.

So this is what losing is like. Drury didn't like it. Even worse than losing, Drury felt handcuffed. He wasn't getting the chance to coach. He was a spectator with an assistant coach name tag.

Drury decided he wasn't going back to Bountiful for another year. But where to go? It turned out that back at Provo High Spencer needed an assistant, so Drury joined his staff in the fall of 1978, the season after Devin Durrant finished off a remarkable high school career and led Provo to a state championship.

Provo now had its heir apparent. When Spencer retired in 1982, Drury made one of the toughest transitions in all of coaching. He went from assistant coach to head coach.

"Stew Morrill (Utah State coach) used to tell me that 18 inches is the biggest move you can make in coaching," Drury said.

Drury made the move and has been a fixture at Provo ever since.

His 362 victories is a mountain of wins, but still an Everest away from Utah's winningest coach, Wilbur Braithwaite of Manti, who has 534 career wins in his career. Larry Maxwell of Highland won 503 games. He's followed by Dugway's George Bruce with 482. Jim Yerkovich of Judge and Spencer both had 478 wins.

"I'll never have as many wins as (Larry) Maxwell or the coaches who have the most wins. I have five state championships; it's not the most but it's the second most," Drury said. "I don't have ego, I don't have to win seven or ten. I don't think you can ever win without talent. We've had kids that can play."

Drury has had his share of great players. Within the last five years, he's had two players (Mekeli Wesley and Jake Chrisman) who have played at BYU.

But when viewing Provo's program under a microscope, what is discovered are two ingredients—good coaching and stability.

"Provo has had just five coaches since 1920. Glen Simmons, Dolan Condie, Jim Spencer and me. Randy Clark took it for one year, in between Simmons and Condie, but that's pretty amazing," Drury said. "I always wanted that picture with Glen, Dolan, Jim, and myself. We established that we were a top program, then Dolan definitely enhanced it. With Jim it was the pinnacle, and I think I've been able to maintain it. Timpview is a spin-off."

Other coaches have looked on in awe and wanted to be part of Provo's family tree.

Despite all of his success and all the great players he's coached, none of his players has ever received "Mr. Basketball," and he has never won "Coach of the Year."

"The players don't get awards because it's the system," Drury said. "And the coaches don't get awards because people say, 'Look at those players.' So it's a double-edged sword. But if the players are so damn good, then why aren't they winning any awards?"

Like any good coach, Drury fights for his players. He wants them to get the recognition they have earned.

When asked what year he did his best coaching job, Drury didn't point to a state championship trophy. He singled out the 1994 team, when Provo took third in state. He's long since gotten over the slight he felt as a younger coach. He's at peace with himself. He doesn't need a plaque to assure himself that he can coach.

Other coaches are constantly trying to pick up some tips on the Drury way. He could author his own book on coaching.

Chapter One - How to handle parents.

"In my parent meeting at the first of the year, I tell them flat out that I'm wrong. In your mind I'm going to be wrong, but my job is to make the decisions. Your job is to be their parents," he says. "I guarantee you if I'm doing my job, your son is going to come home disappointed and hurt about something, maybe something a coach said, or something that happened during the year. Your job is to help him deal with that. There will also be some times when he is excited and something positive has happened."

Chapter Two - Working with big men.

Coaches wonder aloud, "How is it that Provo always has good bigs?"

Timpview coach Perry Wildeboer said, "Drury always does a great job. He'll go down as probably the best post-player coach in Utah history."

Chapter Three - Don't get close to the players or their parents.

He doesn't attend the team dinners that the players organize each week. None of the coaches do.

Chapter Four - Defense.

Drury is perhaps best known for two things. If he were trying to get a college or NBA job, the first thing on his resume would be his two biggest strengths—defense and developing big men.

"Everything has to have a category. If you have to put it in a category, I'd call it a 'matchup-man,'" Drury said of his defense.

If you want more, buy the book.

Now Drury knows he's obsessed, well maybe there's another word for it—competitive. He coaches the way he played. He knows he could spend less time on basketball in the summer. He could cut back in the spring, let someone else coach the team in May. He could skip open gym once in a while, but he doesn't. He could take the whole month of June off, but he won't let himself do it.

One night after a game he sat in a chair in the office and confessed with a sigh, "Provo basketball is part of my life. Maybe too much."

It's what he knows. It's what has family has grown up around, which would explain why a son-in-law has bunk beds made of old Provo bleachers.

From Hollie, his youngest daughter, on up the ladder, from Cassie, Malinda to Rackele, from Becky to Jenifer, all the way to his 82-year old mother, Louise, his family is never far from the bench.

Louise never misses a Provo game. She usually sits a few rows behind Provo's bench and keeps score on a small notepad.

"It's a habit," Louise says. "It helps me from getting so nervous."

Provo's Kade Koop scores in the JV game. She marks down two points for Koop. "Woo, hoo!" she shouts.

This is Drury's life. There are other interests besides basketball. He often goes to the movies with Robin, and if you catch him at a leisure moment, he's probably working on a crossword puzzle.

It helps pass the time when he can't sleep, and as a coach, that is quite often. When the team was in Hawaii, he'd usually get up at 4 a.m. to think. By 6 a.m. he would be on a lawn chair by the beach with a warm ocean breeze blowing through his hair, the only sound is the waves hitting the rocks at high tide. With Hawaiian shorts matched with a gold shirt with blue and white pinstripes, he'd peer through his glasses at his crossword puzzle.

Some of the same things that have made Utah Jazz coach Jerry Sloan so successful in the NBA have made Drury a winner in high school. Mainly it is his competitiveness. He is firm and direct. He can be tough and stern.

One time when he was trying to rent a van from a car rental agency in Hawaii, the agency wouldn't accept the high school's tax exempt number. Drury went to bat for the discount like he goes to bat for one of his players.

A manager came out of the back office to try and settle the issue and said, "This is a tax number from Utah. You are in the state of Hawaii. It says right here it's only good for business in Utah."

A calm but firm Drury replied, "I understand that, but let me tell you my concerns. Why is it that when we go to Florida, Nevada, or Idaho we don't pay sales tax? We've been to tournaments in Oahu and didn't pay sales tax. We were going to go with Alamo, who would have taken our sales tax number, but now we come over here and your rate suddenly is much higher."

"I can check with our accounting office and if we do take it we can reimburse you," the manager said.

"I don't feel comfortable leaving, because when I walk out this door, it will be the end of it," Drury added.

The manager assured him she will look into the matter, but Drury's patience is running out. "Why is it that my Polynesian coach can come in here and get whatever he wants, but because I'm white, you stick it to me? This is an agreement that all states have with each other. We are a high school. We shouldn't have to pay sales tax."

Drury has worked hard fundraising the money for the trip and paying sales tax on the vehicles is a cost he didn't plan on.

Assistant coach Jeff Schoonover waited in the wings and listened to the conversation. "This is how he is with the refs," he said. "He doesn't yell, he's just very stern and commands respect. Very seldom do you see him not get his way."

There's another side to Drury and it can often be seen in the basketball office after the game when he often checks his e-mail and finds a funny photo or video clip that someone has sent him.

One night someone sent him a video clip of a soccer game. It showed a referee giving a player a yellow card. The player went berserk at the sight of the yellow card and attacked the referee and knocked him down, then delivered a barrage of punches before someone intervened.

"I'm going to send this to Caesar (Cardoso), the boys soccer coach," he said with a laugh.

Whether it's getting some athletic tape and taping Schoonover's broken clipboard back together so he won't notice, or talking about who snores the loudest, after wins there's usually laughter in the coaches office as they trade stories.

Drury's never lost the competitive edge that made him successful as a player, but that doesn't mean he's not graceful in defeat. The two don't go hand and hand, but he's been able to win like a winner and lose like one as well.

One instance came during a key region game when Provo was playing Springville in the early 1990s. The Bulldogs trailed 15-7 in the first quarter, but stormed back to take control of the game with a 21-2 run in the second quarter.

By the start of the fourth quarter, Provo had the game put away. But then a bizarre incident took place. Up 20 points with 30 seconds left in the game, Drury stormed onto the court.

He was quickly hit with a technical foul. *What the?*

It's easy to rush to judgment, dismissing Drury as a jerk. But before the game, Springville coach Russ Zaugg asked Drury that if the game was decided if he would do him a favor. Zaugg wanted Todd Frischknecht, their team leader, who was out with a broken leg, to shoot some free throws.

So Drury got a technical.

"I was glad I could do it for them. After all, that's what this game is all about—kids feeling good about themselves," Drury explained of the incident.

He's also helped many of his own kids over the years. There have been kids who didn't have the money to attend tournaments and summer league games who would be lost without the discipline of basketball.

"No question he's a players' coach," said Davis coach Jay Welk. "He doesn't worry about things he can't control, and I don't think he second-guesses himself. Another thing is he has a lot of loyal people around him and he shows a lot of loyalty."

It's all part of his philosophy.

"You know what the definition of a bad kid is? The one you don't know," Drury says.

But he is a coach, and all coaches will eventually do one thing—make enemies.

A few years ago, a woman wanted him fired when Drury supported his freshman coaches after her son was cut. The woman told Provo principal Sam Jarman that Drury verbally abused her on the phone and wanted him fired.

On rare occasions, he swears, and like all coaches he's had years where he's struggled. There have been groups he's coached that he couldn't connect with.

Even on this year's team, Stringham says not everyone on the team likes him. "I guess they don't like it when he gets on them, but I like him. I think he's a good guy and a good coach. I guess they haven't had someone get on them before."

Former player B.J. Chandler, who graduated in 1994, remembers Drury kicking a garbage can across the room once, but says he never swore at them.

Drury doesn't spend time dwelling on the past. When asked what was his most difficult season as a coach, Drury won't say.

"I'm not going to tell you which year that was. I don't want it in the book, but they took third that year, and sometimes I had to get on them."

But over the years, the good years have clearly outweighed the bad. He is now the school's athletic director and says he could be just as happy giving up coaching and being the school's athletic director.

So that begs the question—how much longer will he coach? Not even he knows. If there were a betting line, the over/under would be until 2006, but as it is with all sports bets, there is no sure thing.

"I have a good principal so it's not going to happen now, but if I didn't, if there was something that happened, I would just walk. I'm to that point. I don't need to put up with it. Unless it was something I thought was worth fighting for, I would just walk."

Fortunately for Provo, Drury has a solid cast of assistant coaches that is led by Keli Lobendahn, who has been Drury's assistant since 1990.

Few people call him Coach Lobendahn. The preferred title is coach Keli. Coach Keli was born in Samoa, which sounds like a different county when you hear him say it—Saw-mo-ah. Lobendahn also lived in Fiji.

At age 24, he converted to The Church of Jesus Christ of Latter-day Saints and went to BYU-Hawaii, where he played basketball. He married and started a family.

The Lobendahns moved to Orem in 1989 and he volunteered to coach basketball at Mountain View High School. He then joined Provo volleyball coach Wendy Bills as an assistant and became invaluable to the volleyball program.

Drury kept a watchful eye on Lobendahn and when he had an opening on his staff, he approached Lobendahn about helping with basketball.

Coach Keli agreed and has been Drury's right-hand man ever since.

"He's the guy who stabilizes the players and stabilizes me. He keeps me from getting too high and too low. He's so even keel. He's *my* first assistant," Drury said. "Every high school coach should have a Coach Keli on their staff. He's made me a better overall coach and a better overall person."

Lobendahn teaches at Amelia Earhart Elementary School in Orem and is working on a master's degree in counseling. At times during the season his degree comes in handy.

Coach Keli may be considered Drury's first assistant, but it's Jeff Schoonover that is the junior varsity coach and the one that's most likely to replace Drury when that day comes.

Like Lobendahn, he has a preferred name—most people simply call him Schooney.

Schooney joined Drury's staff in 2000 after he graduated from BYU.

He graduated in 1993 from Pleasant Grove High School where he played basketball. He's married with two children under age three. His brother Danny played baseball at Utah Valley State College and is now the head baseball coach at Lone Peak High School.

Schooney wants to get into administration. If he does, that will end his coaching career, because most school districts won't let a person do both.

"By the time he (Drury) quits, I'll probably be in administration. I've got to do it now while my kids are young. I just can't imagine ever getting out of it (coaching)," Schooney says. "People call up and want to talk to me, but I don't even listen. I don't think I could be an assistant under a lot of coaches, but I can under Drury."

His schedule is draining during the basketball season. He gets up at 5 a.m. to get to his early morning Driver's Ed class. By the time practice ends and he gets home, it's 6 p.m. (on the late days), and by then his wife would like some help with the kids. His younger child had health problems and didn't sleep much at night, which explains why Schooney occasionally lets out a well-justified yawn.

Drury has two other assistants. Cory Green, the sophomore coach, who teaches at the high school, and volunteer assistant Brad Corbitt, who is a BYU student who called Drury and asked if he could help.

Provo head coach Craig Drury (right) and assistant coach Jeff Schoonover look on during a game.

Green moved to Utah from Iowa, where he worked as the assistant high school girls coach for a year and spent two years as the freshman boys coach.

Green is the only non-Mormon on the staff. It's different living among predominately Mormon (LDS) people. Everyone assumes you're a Mormon. He has lost count how many times he's been asked what ward he is in. He usually says something like "the 445th."

One night a woman knocked on his door. Green's wife answered and the woman said she had a sick child and wanted to know if they had any oil.

Green's wife came back with some Crisco.

"No, like consecrated (healing) oil," the woman said.

After a few minutes, Green's wife come back with some olive oil.

Then the woman realized her mistake. "You aren't LDS are you?"

Despite the cultural differences, Green is happy coaching at Provo. Even though the sophomores are experiencing their first losing season since he's been the coach, Green says this year has been his best. He's been challenged and has had to take himself off "auto pilot" and dig deep down.

Corbitt is from Southern California. He played for Vanais High School with Casey Jacobsen, who is now with the Phoenix Suns.

He doesn't want to get into coaching. He's hoping for a law degree. He brings a unique perspective to the program, mostly enthusiasm. He's BYU's biggest fan. He came to practice on Feb. 5th, national letter of intent day, pumped up to talk about two lineman who signed at BYU.

"After BYU lost to Utah, I went down on the field and watched Utah fans take down the goal posts. I was the last to leave. I just sat there in tears," Corbitt said.

The same enthusiasm he has for BYU, he brings to practice. Corbitt will often run drills with the team and even do pushups when someone scores on him.

He'll pick out players to yell at.

"Here we go, Groesbeck."

"Way to play defense, Joey."

One day he came in and said, "Did you see the baseball score?"

Baseball? In the end of January?

"Yeah, BYU beat Arizona in the first game, but then they lost the next two. They got beat 32-3 in the final game, the most runs they have ever given up."

Later in practice he prepares for his law degree by debating the superiority of BYU's athletic program over that of Utah's.

When asked about BYU's upcoming basketball game at Utah, Corbitt says, "BYU at Utah, I think BYU will win by double figures, something like 12 points or more."

Utah won by seven (71-64) to sweep the season series against BYU, but you would never know it. When he's asked about the game at practice, he shows the same optimism. He just changes the subject to the NCAA tournament.

This is Drury's staff. None of them are likely to be his successors, which may be one reason why Drury has set no timetable on when he will give it up. He's told others he won't go until there's a coach ready to take over, until he knows the program is in good hands, but that may not be possible.

So when asked about retiring, Drury says not even he knows when he'll quit. Maybe when the rewards don't outweigh the time. Maybe when the kids he coaches are no longer interested in working hard.

Maybe that day will never come.

Drury's son-in-law, Chad Shumway, is the assistant basketball coach at Blanding High School (Utah).

Drury says, "I've told my wife, 'someday I'm going to assist him and be kind of like his Keli Lobendahn.' He has some of the attributes I wish I had. He's an excellent coach."

But Drury doesn't dream of the future or dwell in the past. There is very little in his west Provo home that would indicate he is one of the winningest coaches in Utah history. You have to go inside his bedroom to find any basketball memorabilia. It's on a high shelf above his bedroom door that even he has to strain to reach where he keeps five autographed basketballs from the state championship teams. He also has a few plaques.

To quote one of Drury's favorite people, Henry Ford, "History is for losers."

"Those that dwell in history, that's where you are," Drury says. I want to be the 2003 state champions, but it won't help me get there by thinking about the 1998 state championship."

For Drury, there is glory in the past, but there is promise in the future.

CHAPTER 4

ALOHA

Any reference to "Aloha" brings Hawaii to mind. So what does that have to do with Provo?

In a day of cutbacks and layoffs, in an era of shared textbooks and teachers dipping into their own pockets to buy luxuries such as pencils and paper, how in the world could a high school basketball team even think about taking such a frivolous trip to Hawaii?

Oh, there was one other thing. What would a trip to Hawaii be without the cheerleaders?

Yep, they're coming too.

Inquiring coaches would like to know, not to mention the President of the Utah Education Association.

Here's how it happened. Drury went to the school board and presented his case in July of 2002. "I would like to take my basketball team to Hawaii," he said. "There may be some cheerleaders who come, too."

It took a few minutes for the laughter to die down. The board was less than enthusiastic.

Time to vote. All in favor?

One timid hand goes up.

All opposed? Four.

Aloha meant "goodbye, Hawaii." But just because the school board sent Provo a resounding "No," doesn't mean the game was over. Provo simply trailed at the half and Drury saved his starters for the second half.

He sent Dave Hagen, Mick's father, to talk to the school board as a representative of the players' parents.

"We want this trip. It's good for the kids," Hagen argued. "Are you going to tell us what he can do with our kids? The money will be raised."

Time for a revote.All opposed?

None.

All in favor?

Unanimous.

Aloha now meant "pack your bags."

The one thing Provo had going for it was history. The Bulldogs had gone to Hawaii three times before. In 1997, Provo had four players on the team with Hawaii connections and combined with assistant coach Keli Lobendahn's ties to the islands, Provo got an invitation to the Iloni Classic. Provo finished second in the 1997 tournament, which led to future invitations to the tournament in 1998 and in 2000. The Bulldogs took second again in 1998 and finished fifth in 2000.

The competition in Hawaii attracted some of the elite teams in the country. The 2000 tournament included Dominguez High School from Compton, California. Dominguez featured Tyson Chandler, the second overall pick in the 2001 draft by the Chicago Bulls. The tournament also included Washington Union High School in Fresno, California, which featured DeShawn Stevenson, first round pick of the Utah Jazz in the 2000 draft.

Having gone to Hawaii three times in four years, Provo sent a signal that times were officially changing. Traveling to play in out-of-state tournaments was virtually unheard of 20 years ago, but now it's routine for many of the top teams to travel out of state.

Provo was one of the first teams in Utah to travel. In 1982, former Provo coach Jim Spencer accepted an invitation to play in the Scorpion Classic in Farmington, New Mexico. The Bulldogs won the tournament and started a new tradition.

When Spencer retired, Drury continued to attend the Scorpion Classic, where the Bulldogs won the tournament nine years in a row and put together a 29-game winning streak in the tournament before finally losing.

Provo went back to the Scorpion Classic in 1996, but it would be the final trip to New Mexico for the Bulldogs.

Traveling is now a good thing at Provo; the Bulldogs go somewhere every year. In 1999 the team went to a tournament in Atlanta, and after the trip to Hawaii in 2000, Provo went to Fort Lauderdale, Florida in 2001. In 2003, Provo will return to Fort Lauderdale.

Over the years, Provo has posted a 48-8 record in tournaments outside of Utah, proving what other teams in Utah already know—Provo has one of the elite high school basketball programs in the country.

So even though history was on its side, Provo still had to clear some hurdles to go back to Hawaii. The team wanted to leave on a Tuesday, which would mean the players would miss two and a half days of school. That was too much, so a compromise was worked out. The team would leave on Wednesday and miss only a day and a half of school. That was more like it, especially considering the benefits. A trip to Hawaii was the opportunity of a lifetime. Call it geography extra credit.

Drury now had permission, but he'd also just signed up for a major undertaking. There's a reason why other teams don't go to Hawaii. He had 18 players, two of the team's stat girls, three coaches, and a trainer to cover expenses for. It was something that doesn't usually fall in a coach's job description.

The players were asked to come up with $500 each. Drury would figure out a way to cover the rest. The team hosted a luau, but that only raised about $500. So Drury went to businesses run by Provo alumni and asked for $150 to $400. In one day he raised $1,100 from three businesses.

Drury's mother donated $3,000, and he got another $5,000 from an anonymous donor.

Even though Drury had fundraised the additional money it would take to pay the remainder of the tab, there was still at least one player who couldn't come up with the $500. No worries, Drury had work for him to do so he could earn the money.

The cheerleaders took a slightly different approach. Since they weren't required to go, they were on their own to raise money for their entire trip. They teamed up with the players for a free-throw shooting contest where players would shoot 200 free throws and cheerleaders asked fellow students or friends to donate money to the cause for each free throw the player made.

There were other ways the cheerleaders raised money. Some

offered to clean houses or cook dinners (no refunds) or even offer massages.

With the money raised and the accommodations secured, the players, cheerleaders, and advisors met at the school at 3:30 a.m. on Wednesday, December 18.

Joining the players and coaches were a handful of parents that included Pututau's mother; Mick Hagen's parents and younger brother; Scott Ady's mother, father, and older brother; Mercer's parents and older brother Glade, who played at Provo in 1999; Wesley's parents, younger brother and sister; and Lobendahn's daughter.

None of the coaches brought their wives. Drury says such a trip is 90 percent work (80 percent of that is supervising) and 10 percent vacation, not exactly the ratio a wife would appreciate.

By the time the team landed in Maui and arrived at the condo in Lahaina, it was 4 p.m. Maui time. Within minutes after arriving at the condo, players were already scattered along the beach. Steve Torkildson, who lost 26 pounds in three weeks on an all-protein, no-carbohydrate diet, had to hold on to his swimming suit with one hand to keep it from falling down.

Coach Keli wasted no time walking down to the beach, which is a stone's throw from the condo. Within 10 minutes a half dozen players followed Lobendahn down the beach. They learned more in a hour with him than they will in a semester in biology at school.

Within a hundred yards of the condo, Lobendahn found a crab, a sea urchant and several limpets. He pointed out a man who was snorkeling and harvesting antler seaweed.

"They put that on salads," Lobendahn explained. "You have to leave three or four inches so it will grow back."

There's more sights to see. Lobendahn found a sea anemone and another crab, which he picked up and showed the players how to hold it without getting pinched.

Back at team headquarters, the coaches' condo, Drury makes the itinerary for the day. Now that the team is in Maui, Drury has to be careful the team doesn't shift into party mode and forget about the reason they came in the first place.

With a 6 p.m. game, Drury fears the team will stay up late and sleep in, so he schedules a 6 a.m. shootaround on Thursday morning.

After the shootaround, the players are on their own until they start getting ready at 4 p.m. Most stay close to the condo. Some lounge by the condo pool. Others walk along the beach and many play Nintendo or video games they have hooked up to the TVs in their rooms.

The first game of the tournament is against Huntington Beach, (California). Lahainaluna High School is the host school for the six-team tournament. Lahainaluna High is perched on the side of the mountain with a post-card-worthy view of the ocean.

Provo has never seen Huntington Beach play and knows nothing about the California team, but does it matter?

Provo doesn't worry about what other teams do. The Bulldogs play Provo defense and stick with their game plan—pound the ball inside.

Huntington Beach jumps out to a 6-4 lead, but Provo comes back to go up 12-11 after a steal and basket by Hagen at the end of the first quarter.

The second quarter is a disaster for the Bulldogs. Assistant coach Jeff Schoonover thinks the shootaround at 6 a.m. kicked in. The team is playing tired. The only basket of the quarter comes on a Cory Carter steal and layup. The rest of the quarter is a exhibition in futility. Pututau misses a three. Hagen takes a long three and misses. The team fouls are lopsided—ten for Provo and just five for Huntington Beach—and Tika Wesley nearly gets into a fight with a Huntington Beach player in a bizarre incident early in the second quarter.

A player on Huntington Beach punched Tika with a clenched fist in the groin three times. Finally Tika retaliated by pushing the player and shouting at him. He made a fist and was ready to punch the player, but before he could, a double foul was called.

"What are you doing?" Tika asked the player, then he added, "I'm going to knock you out."

The response from the Huntington Beach player was, "Go ahead. You'll be out of the game and we'll take home the trophy."

The incident does nothing to fire up Provo. The team retreats to the wrestling room upstairs where Drury's competitive juices are boiling. His comments are mainly aimed at his guards.

"Joey, you don't shoot it like that in practice. Do you want to

Assistant coach Keli Lobendahn holds up a crab that he found while walking the beach.

shoot? I can put a No. 55 on you and have coach work with you on post moves."

Pututau looks down at the floor and takes his scolding. He occasionally looks up at Drury and nods his head.

Now it's Hagen's turn.

"Mick, if this is just a resume filler, we'll be better without you. You've got to play with some energy, some intensity."

Drury's message gets through. The Bulldogs respond and look like a completely different team in the third quarter as they start the second half with a 16-2 run.

Tai Wesley opens the scoring in the quarter with a three-point play. Stringham then comes up with a steal and feeds Hagen for two. Tika then scores inside and Carter pops a three-pointer. Stringham pulls down an offensive rebound and is fouled. He drops in two free throws. Tika and Corbin Mercer both hit a pair of free throws to push Provo's lead to 29-21 with 2:01 left in the quarter.

Huntington Beach closes the gap to 32-27 at the end of the third quarter, but Pututau doesn't let Huntington Beach come back. He scores all 10 of his points in the final quarter to help Provo hold on for a 54-42 win.

Hagen leads the team in scoring with 15 points. Tika adds 12 points, and Carter chips in with eight as the team improves to 4-0.

After the game, while the scores are called into the newspapers back home, Drury makes it a point to mention what a good second half Hagen played.

The win is cause for celebration. The Wesley family has agreed to host the team for dinner. There is an outdoor kitchen and a mini pavilion next to the pool where the dinner is served. The Wesleys serve up a combination of pork, noodles, and rice and even dessert.

It's definitely a Kodak moment. The tiki lights surround the pool as the sound of waves breaking on the beach serenades the team. The ocean is less than fifty yards away. Stars dot the sky, and off in the distance a cruise ship is parked for the night.

The team breaks up into groups of three to five, sometimes just two, and scatter along the beach. Coach Keli eats some of the day's catch. He splits the limpets with Hiagi Wesley and then gets Corbin and Stringham to try some limpets. Stringham shrugs his shoulders and says, "It's okay," but Mercer doesn't agree. He wipes his hand on the bricks by the pool and looks for something to drink to help wash away the taste.

※※※

Next up for Provo is a game against Waimea, a local team from the island of Kauai. Its clear after a few minutes that Waimea is undersized and should be no match for the Bulldogs.

They advanced to the second round after jumping on another island team 47-7 in the first half. Schoonover scouted the game and says the other team looked like a bunch of guys (munchkins) from the Wizard of Oz.

Waimea is respectable. They have a football lineman inside to battle the Wesleys and a three-point specialist that keeps the team in games, along with a tough, quick 6'3" slasher that could shoot outside or drive to the hole.

Still, Waimea has a problem—it doesn't have the depth it needs to hang with Provo. The Bulldogs take a 27-14 lead at the half thanks in large part to Pututau, who looks relaxed and confident. He hit four 3-pointers in the first half to give the Bulldogs a commanding lead.

But the killer instinct is still on the beach, taking one more wave. Waimea comes back to cut the lead to 34-29 at the end of the third quarter. It would be an embarrassment to lose to this team, not to mention ruining the trip.

Hagen opens the quarter with a crucial three-pointer. Waimea answers with a bucket. Tika then hits two free throws, and Pututau comes up with a steal and follows with a three-pointer to put the Bulldogs up 42-31 with 5:30 left to play in the game.

Provo holds on for a 52-40 win and advances to the championship of the tournament, but the win doesn't please the coaching staff.

"That was an awful display of basketball," Drury says. "Mick, are you hearing what I'm saying? You're the leader of this group. The ball is not moving and no one is coming to the ball. I wish you could see the film to know what I'm talking about. People say there is no 'I' in team. That's a misnomer. There is an 'I' in team. The 'I' is I've got to do my job."

One of the players who should have had a big game against the undersized Waimea team is Tai, but he was a non-factor.

"Tai, I want you to be the first one to the car, not the last. You haven't done anything yet. You've had one decent game and you're walking around all cocky," Drury says. "If I had to rate the way we played, I'd give you a C- or a D+ on offense and I'd give you about the same on defense. I was going to take tomorrow off and skip the shootaround. Bull crap. We're going to have a shootaround."

The coaches' theory behind Tai's struggles are believed to be linked to his roommates. Tai had missed two layups in the first half, but responded with nine rebounds and eight points in the second half after getting singled out by Drury.

Tai's three roommates, juniors Garrett Groesbeck, Eric Walker, and Dustin Migliaccio weren't likely to play in the tournament. While they stayed up late and played around, Tai followed their lead.

But there was another factor. Thursday night Tai kissed one of the cheerleaders in the group. So? She was teammate Jordan Snarr's girlfriend. Sparks would soon fly and angry words would be exchanged. A feud was underway between the two players, and weren't even speaking to each other. But before they left Hawaii, peace was restored and the two put it behind them.

Drury isn't the only coach who's disappointed with the team's effort. Coach Keli says, "I'm not worried about this game. I'm worried about not being one of the four teams that makes the playoffs from our region. There's never been a Provo team that didn't make the playoffs, but this could be the first. We're not playing like we're going to be one of them. Spanish Fork will beat us."

The good news is the team is now 5-0 and has advanced to the championship round of the tournament. After taking the players back to the condo, the coaches go back to the high school later that night to scout Mayfield, the team expected to play Provo for the title.

After watching the first half Drury says, "We'll beat them. We'll beat these guys. They're good at pressuring the ball, but they can't shoot. No. 14 is their only shooter."

The coaches then celebrate the win at Bubba Gump's Shrimp restaurant where they unwind by answering *Forrest Gump* trivia questions with the waitress.

When they return to the condo, the rooms are empty. Most of the players are on the beach with the cheerleaders. Schoonover is sent to tell them about shootaround.

"Okay, you guys need to go to bed. We're shooting around tomorrow at 10. Get to bed."

The group breaks up and Schoonover heads back to his room. Five minutes later he makes a room check. All accounted for but Hagen, who is on a moonlit walk with one of the cheerleaders named Heidi.

Schoonover finally finds Hagen and ends their night by escorting him back to the room and tells the players, "The next wave is coach Keli. After that is coach Drury and he's ornery. He'd kill you."

The players don't want to have the next wave come.

※※※

Provo made it to the championship game where they would meet Mayfield High School from Orange County, California, who came into the game with a record of 6-1.

This is the type of team Drury was hoping to play in Hawaii. They are quick, athletic, and have the size to matchup with Provo.

Playing Mayfield is the perfect test for the preseason. Unlike the game against Waimea, Provo is up for this game from the opening tip.

Hagen and Carter hit three-pointers and Tai Wesley converts a three-point play. Chris Childress, Mayfield's 6'6" shooting forward, is held to just two points, but a balanced Mayfield team gets others to step up and leave the score tied at nine after the first quarter.

Mayfield then takes control in the second quarter. Tai misses a pair of contested layups inside, while Childress erupts for seven points in the quarter. Pututau has four points and Tika has the other two as the Bulldogs trail 19-16 at the end of the half.

In the third quarter Provo responds with a 7-0 run to start the second half. The Bulldogs pound Mayfair inside and get a three-point play from Tika, a layup from Tai, and another bucket from Tika to take a 30-27 lead into the fourth quarter.

Provo runs into trouble early in the the fourth quarter when Stringham joins Tika in foul trouble with four. Tai is called for a travel and Carter has his layup blocked. Mayfair's Brian McFadden then makes a shake-and-bake move and blows past Hagen for a layup. Another Provo turnover and a three-pointer by Arnie Hollis gives Mayfair a 32-30 lead with 5:10 left in the game.

Steve Torkildson tied the game when he pulled down an offensive rebound and was fouled. He swished one free throw and after a timeout dropped in another free throw. But Justin Hawkins of Mayfair hit a three-pointer with four minutes left to put Provo down three at 35-32.

Then came the shot of the game. Hagen hit a three-pointer from the wing and then hit the floor. The whistle blew. Three plus one! A rare four-point play gives the Bulldogs a 36-35 lead with 3:17 left to play. Pututau then delivered the knockout blow. He followed with a three-pointer. After Pututau's shot tickled the twine, Drury danced a jig in front of Provo's bench and let out a "Yeah!" That should answer any question about whether the flame to coach still burns in Drury's heart after 20 years of being a head coach.

Sensing he had Mayfair on the ropes, Drury went to the spread offense after Stringham pulled down a Mayfair miss with two minutes left in the game. Provo would either shoot free throws or take a layup.

Mayfair opted to foul and put Pututau on the line. He hit one of two free throws. After McFadden hit two free throws for Mayfair to cut the lead back to three with 1:43 remaining, Hagen then found a three-pointer from the top of the key too irresistible. Talk about pressure. Not because Provo was up by just three in the championship game with a minute left. No, the pressure came in a different form. If Hagen missed the 23-foot shot, Drury may not forgive him until his kids' kids came through the program.

Swish.

Whew!

Provo finished off Mayfair at the free-throw line. Hagen canned four straight free throws, then Tika made two, and Kade Koop hit one of two to preserve the win.

The result was an impressive 49-37 win. Afterward the team celebrated like a scaled-down state championship. They gave each other high fives and hugs. Hagen and Pututau posed for a picture. The cheerleaders joined the team for a picture on center court as they handed out candy leis to the players.

The trophy was a hand carved tiki (means "the first man") that weighed about 40 pounds and had 2002 tournament champs carved on it. The team passed the unique trophy around for everyone to handle.

Meanwhile, the tournament director collected and counted the votes from other coaches and announced the all-tournament team.

Pututau was the first Provo player named to the all-tournament team. He averaged 11.3 points per game. Hagen was chosen as the tournament MVP. He led the team in scoring for each game with 15, 16, and 17 points per game.

To show you how different coaches view the game, Drury and Schoonover say Tika, who averaged 10.3 points per game and was the key to the team's inside attack, should have been on the all-tournament team if not the MVP. They also say Stringham, who scored four points in each of the first two games and none in the championship game, should have gotten all-tournament honors. Stringham had five rebounds in the championship game and played inspired defense.

The win leaves everyone in a good mood. The Hagen family buys dessert and offers cheesecake and key lime pie to all comers on the beach.

Mick and Heidi take another walk and Torkildson and Jackie, who have just started dating, take a walk on the beach.

The next day is Sunday and Drury says, "I'm going to church. If you want to come, be at the vans at 10:15."

About half of the team comes and a few cheerleaders show up for the service. After church is out, the players spend the rest of the day lounging on the lawn chairs by the beach.

Hagen, Pututau and Ady all go with their families on a drive to see the Creator, one of Maui's most popular attractions. The Creator is actually called Haleakala, an active volcano that is a spectacular site.

A 26-mile windy road takes cars to over 10,000 feet. The players are joined by a handful of cheerleaders, who take a different van.

The final day, a Monday, the team members check out of their condos and head for Fleming's Beach, a few miles down the road where the surf is up and the sand is white.

Finally, the players can go all out and not worry about being ready to play. They can body surf and play football and not worry about getting ready for a game, and they take advantage of it.

Torkildson volunteers to get buried in the sand by Jackie and three other cheerleaders, Natalie, Tara, and Heidi.

Jordan Snarr figures the girls need some help, so he's on hand to make sure Torkildson is buried deep enough to keep him from moving.

After 20 minutes of getting buried, Torkildson breaks out of the sand and he finds out something is wrong. He believes he had an allergic reaction to the sand, because the fingers on both hands swell up like a badly sprained ankle. The lifeguard pours vinegar over his fingers, but it doesn't work. Torkildson believes something bit him, but he never found out what it was.

Soon the team gets a football game going on the beach. It's not regular football, it's pass anywhere. Once you kickoff, you can keep

Provo celebrates after beating Mayfair High School of southern California to win the Maui tournament.

passing the ball forward or backward until you're tackled or until a pass is incomplete.

To ensure there are no injuries, the players decide to play touch, unless you're in the water, in which case it's all-out tackle.

They play for 25 minutes without incident. Snarr shows why he started at defensive back on the football team. He picks off three passes in a matter of minutes.

The game finally ends when junior Kade Koop gets the ball and races up the sideline and into the waves. He is now fair game. Stringham tracks him down and pile drives Koop into the surf with a textbook tackle.

Koop is down for the count. He struggles to regain his balance in the surf and immediately checks his teeth. "Are my teeth in? My teeth got knocked out," Koop says as he feels his bottom teeth for damage.

His teammates, including Stringham, assure him his bottom teeth are all there. Well all, but half of a bottom tooth.

"Sorry, man. You okay? " Stringham asks.

Koop wants no part of the apology. He shakes his head and walks toward the sand. Game over. It's time to eat anyway, so the players, cheerleaders, and coaches load the vans and head for a shopping area that is close to several restaurants.

Koop's half tooth is soon singing in pain. He's in luck. Laura, one of the stat keepers, has some prescription pain pills with her.

"Just take a half of one," she tells him.

Somehow that's translated into "Take two."

Koop is soon in la-la land. While in the back of the van on the way to a restaurant, Koop tells everyone, "Valerie (the other stat girl) kissed me."

"Valerie is not even in the van," Schoonover says.

Schoonover later finds out Koop did get a kiss on the cheek to help ease the pain, but it's clear Koop has no concept of time. He just speaks what's on his mind.

"Valerie kissed me."

Earth to Kade Koop.

The team shows up at the Hardrock Cafe to eat lunch. The waitress asks, "Table for . . ."

"About 35."

Scott Ady (left) and Tai Wesley (right) ride a wave in at Fleming's Beach in Maui.

She laughs, but this is no joke. The team takes up half of the restaurant. Once they're seated, Schoonover and Drury focus on Koop.

Schoonover takes Koop into the bathroom to try and get him to throw up, but he can't do it. Since they're not sure what to do, they call trainer Donnie Bills and Koop's parents in an effort to solve the situation.

Meanwhile, Drury has a talk with Laura at one of the tables. He uses a direct but quiet tone that no one else could hear unless sitting at their table.

Laura stares down at the table and continues to nod her head while she wipes away the tears. She'll never do that again. Koop will be fine and by the time dinner is over the incident has been forgotten and everyone heads to the nearby shops for some last-minute souvenir shopping.

When Drury planned a trip to Hawaii, he never imagined he would have to deal with something like this. Now it's clear this is no vacation for Drury. This is not his idea of R and R.

Now he must figure out what players are staying in Hawaii and which ones are coming home with the team.

Drury has the group show up at the airport at 7 p.m for an 11:30 p.m. flight. It's early, but that's the idea. "Once I have them at the airport, my job is done," Drury says.

Supervision duties are over.

It looks like Hagen has found his girlfriend. Things went well with Heidi. It turns out Heidi has liked Mick since the 8th grade. She even applied to be his girlfriend after he wrote his column in the school newspaper. It looks like it has finally happened, but she's not sure where they stand. It's time for the talk, you know, the talk about the DTR.

What's a DTR? Come on, where you been? Under a rock? DTR—Define the Relationship.

※※※

After flying all night from Maui to San Francisco, the team arrives in San Francisco at 6 a.m. and prepares for a four-hour layover on what is now Christmas Eve.

Freshman Mark Walker uses the time to come up with the 12 Days in Maui, as he catches the spirit of the season.

On the 12th Day in Maui, this is what you'd see:

12 screaming fans
11 geckos jumping
10 dollars missing
9 footer Tika
8 warm'n benches
7 Pom-poms flying
6 hour practice
5 coconuts
4 point plays
3 awesome coaches
2 Wesleys post'n
and a point guard who strokes a three.

Everyone seems happy. Christmas is only a day away. The players, many of whom have never been away from home this long, will be home for Christmas armed with souvenirs and a renewed love for their families that only a separation can create.

CHAPTER FIVE

THE ADY MILLION DOLLAR QUESTION

Question. Who would purposely choose to move during the summer before their senior year of high school?

Who would leave a place he'd called home for the last 16 years, a place where he was the star, at a school where he averaged 21 points and 11 rebounds, where he had 19 triple-doubles as a junior in 45 games? Who would do this for the uncertainty of playing for another team at another school?

Who would leave to play in a different country? Who would stay when it was clear his role would change from star to sub?

Part A of the eighty million dollar question is, "How much does basketball mean to you?" Part B is, "What do you do after years of playing basketball, but now you are a senior and it's apparent you can chart your playing time with a stop watch and not an hour glass?"

Meet Scott Ady, a lanky, 6'3" lefty from Calgary, Canada. Ady has brown hair but like many athletes his age, he's bleached the top of his head so when he spikes his hair there are streaks of blonde mixed in.

He's only 175 pounds, so it shouldn't be a shock to know that he once ran in the Boston Marathon and that he will participate in track when the basketball season is over.

His best sport isn't basketball, it's volleyball, and when he graduates he would like to walk-on at a college and play volleyball.

Ady was born in Wyoming, but six months later moved to Portland, and by age two the family settled in Calgary, a place Ady would call home.

Ady loved Canada. There was so much to do. His family shared a cabin in Montana, a five-hour drive from Calgary where they spent many weekends and summer nights.

Calgary was unique. It offered incredible skiing, much better than the skiing in Utah, Ady says. There was also the annual Slush Cup, where the locals would build a ski jump that led directly to a pool of icy, slushy water.

"The first time I went off it, I laid out and did a belly flop," Ady said with a laugh. "It hurt and the water was freezing."

Ady had never thought about leaving Canada until he watched a high school basketball game on TV.

Ady's mother, who works in government as a member of the legislative assembly (similar to a senator in the United States), wondered if Scott would like to play in the United States.

There was another reason the Adys wondered if their son was up for a change. He was starting to get into some mischief. He nearly got arrested when he pulled a prank that backfired.

"Me and a buddy took some fishing line and tied it to a door knocker, then strung the line behind some trees," Ady explained. "We kept pulling on it and when the lady came to the door, she couldn't see the fishing line. We did this five times. She was getting freaked out, but then the line broke. We went back to the door to fix the line and when we did, her neighbor came out of the door and started chasing us."

The concerned neighbor thought the two boys were trying to break into the house and called the police.

Within minutes, a police helicopter hovered above and several police cars swarmed the area. Ady and his friend were apprehended and were headed to jail, until their story matched that of the woman whose house was the target of the prank.

Ady wasn't so lucky the next time. He tagged along with a friend to McDonalds one night. He took a video camera to record the event. His friend went wild in the McDonalds, spraying flame retardant from a fire extinguisher all over the restaurant and on the counter.

Needless to say, the manager of McDonalds didn't see any humor in the event and all three were arrested.

Maybe it wasn't a bad idea for Scott to have a change of scenery.

A week after his mother wondered if Scott wanted to take his game to Utah, his father Don brought up the subject again.

Scott's older brother was living in Provo, Utah, attending Brigham Young University. He could stay with him and attend Provo High School.

A call was made and Drury said, "Bring him down."

Ady arrived for three days in May and then came back in the summer, preparing to make the move. Since Ady was still in school in June, he had to make a leap of faith and drop out of school in Canada while he checked out Provo High.

He arrived on a Wednesday and played with Provo in open gym during the summer. By Friday, he was still considered to be the new guy and the only thing anyone said to him was "Hey you."

Ady was too shy to even ask for a ride home, so he would run home after practice, adding another three miles to his workout.

"I called home and told my mom that it wasn't working out. I told her I gave it a shot and wanted to come home," Ady said. "My mom is a pretty spiritual person, so she told me to pray about it. It sounds kind of corny, but I remember it was a Saturday and I prayed about it. About 30 minutes later, Mick and Joe knocked on my door and said, "Scott, right? Do you want to hang out with us?"

Now it's hard to think of Ady as shy. When the team went to a flea market in Hawaii, Ady showed why he may have a future in law.

Under a cabana that was filled with Hawaiian shirts, board shorts, and a variety of shell necklaces, Ady went to work. He picked out five t-shirts. "These five for $22," he tells a Hawaiian lady.

No, is the reply. "$26 dollars."

Is this Tijuana? Ady looks at this as a challenge.

"No, I can only go $22, that's as high as I can go," Ady says.

"$23," the lady counters.

"No, I can only go $22," Ady maintains.

"These are good quality t-shirts," the lady insists.

"I know, that's why I'll go to $22," Ady says.

Frustrated by the bargaining session, the lady sharply replies, "No, $23, take it or leave it."

"Nope, $22," Ady says.

The lady doesn't reply. Ady, still holding the shirts draped over one of this arms, just stares at her with a smile.

A few minutes later he emerges with a sack that has the five T-shirts he picked out.

"Got them for $22," he says with a laugh.

Thirty minutes later, Ady is at it again. The team has gathered at the designated spot that is around a table that has a variety of necklaces. It's lunch time and the flea market is closing and the team in ready to go to lunch. Ady picks up a necklace that has a $12 price tag on it and says, "I'll give you $5."

The answer is no.

"Look, how many of us there are. If you want to sell a lot . . ."

Time runs out on Ady. The team is hungry, but no matter, Ady has already done well. He's well stocked with souvenirs.

The trip to Hawaii was one of mixed emotions for Ady. It was the trip of a lifetime, but it was hard to ignore that while he was in paradise, his role on the team was changing.

Ady played in Provo's first three games of the season, but didn't score a point. He shot two air balls in one game and began losing playing time.

By the time the team went to Hawaii, Ady was out of the rotation and the realization that he had slipped down the depth chart finally sunk in. He was now so far down the bench that Drury would have to put his glasses on to see him.

Ady's parents and older brother made the trip to Maui to watch him play, he didn't play in the first game against Huntington Beach and scored just one point in the team's next game against Kauai. When Provo played Mayfair in the championship game, Ady didn't play a minute.

While the team posed for pictures and passed around the tiki trophy, Ady had a hard time forcing a smile. Sure the team won, but it did it without him.

Back at his room, Ady couldn't hide his disappointment. Tears escaped.

Mick and Joey tried to make him feel better. They wrote "We love you Scott," on their mirror with deodorant.

When the team gathered later, Ady wouldn't make eye contact with Drury.

Drury was aware of Ady's frustration, but if there's one thing he's learned in his years of being a head coach, it's that you can never make everyone happy.

"It's not my job to make people happy. I can't worry about that," Drury says. 'I've got to play the lineup that gives us the best chance of winning. I'm glad he (Schoonover) talked to him (Ady). He's doing what an assistant coach does."

On Sunday, a day after the Bulldogs won the tournament, Drury took a sight-seeing drive to the Haleakala volcano. The drive is one of the most spectacular in all of Hawaii. The road winds from sea level to 10,364 feet in just 26 miles.

There was talk of the team making the drive to the top of the active volcano and riding bikes back down, but by Sunday, most of the players weren't up for a long drive and instead opted to lounge around the condo and visit the beach.

While on top of the world, looking out over a spectacular view of the ocean and an amazing view of the volcano and the lush green valley, Drury ran into the Adys, who had also made the trip along with the Hagen family and Pututau and his mother.

During the sight-seeing outing, Scott's parents approached Drury to ask him about Scott's playing time.

"What are our options?"

Drury responded by saying, "You tell me."

The Adys wondered about the possibility of transferring schools. How could their all-star not be good enough to play five minutes a game?

But not knowing the rules in Utah, Ady's parents hoped Drury could tell them what—if anything—Scott could do.

Basically, he was out of luck. Scott couldn't change schools in midseason just because he wasn't getting the playing time he wanted.

As a senior and a move-in, he had just two options. Stick it out or quit.

The real transition for Scott was now at hand. His plight is not uncommon in high school sports. It happens nearly every year at every school.

You can't possibly have a varsity team that consists of 17 players and make everyone happy. It's a basketball fact of life.

Ady had potential, but he was behind. His offense had suffered from limited minutes and when it came to defense, Ady was still in a daze.

"In Canada, it's a completely different game. There's a 30-second shot clock and it's way more up and down, run and gun," Ady explained. "Here you can pass it around for a minute and a half before you take a shot. I just wasn't used to that and the defense was hard, it really threw me. I had to trust in my teammates."

Provo runs such a complicated defense that no one really knows what to call it. When pressed, Drury described it as a match-up man defense. But there's a lot of switching and variations according to what the offense is doing. You just don't show up, practice it a few times, and you are good to go.

Schooney said it wasn't until his third year as an assistant that he felt comfortable enough to teach the defense, and even then he says he wasn't sure all the switching and changes the big men are responsible for.

It took time to put the disappointment in Hawaii behind him, but by the end of the preseason Ady was at peace with the situation and so were his parents. He had good friends and he played on a winning team. Even though he didn't play as much as he would have liked, he finally focused on the positives.

He had made the team! Did he know how big a feat that in itself was? It's actually happened just two other times in Drury's 20 years as head coach.

So this is how Ady's high school career would end, on the bench, hoping the starters would open a big enough lead that Drury would feel safe and put him in. Looking forward to a game against Springville and hoping each time the Bulldogs took the court, they would blow out their opponent so he could play.

Many players in Ady's position would have quit or retreated to home. They would complain about the politics, bemoan the coaching staff. They would spend their time lashing out behind the backs of the coaching staff that may know basketball, but can't judge talent. Then they would launch into a diatribe for anyone that would listen.

But one of the lessons Ady has learned when coming to America was about pride. How to bridle it. How to control it. How to suppress it.

It was during the tournament in Hawaii when Ady faced his moment of truth. How would he handle the situation?

Over time he opted to be a team player; he would dim the lights on his desire to play in the games and pick up the pace in practice. But it was a struggle. There have been tears more than once—wondering why the coaches didn't see him the way he sees himself.

After falling out of the varsity rotation, Drury decided to start him in junior varsity games in an effort for Ady to get some confidence in his shot and get a better handle on his defensive role.

He produced 18 points in one game, but they still didn't see what they were looking for, and once region play began, Ady knew on most nights the only sweat he would be working up would be in practice. But it didn't change his status when it came to the varsity game. He found something amazing happened once he accepted his role—peace.

There is more to playing high school basketball than getting your name in the box score. The basketball experience includes more than just 32 minutes of game time. Just watch Ady sit with his legs stretched out into the aisle of the bus riding back from a game late on Friday night. He can sing. He sings with the rest of the team in harmony. "I'm a Bulldog, I'm a Bulldog, I'm a Bulldog till I die . . . ."

He would win the Scrub Cup. He would find friends that shared his same values. He would see the game from a different point of view and watch his senior year go by from the bench.

"I have to admit, I thought about quitting the team," Ady said. "What has kept me playing is the social life. I don't get to play much, I can't change that, so I thought I might as well make it a positive. I'm hoping one game we'll get up and I can get a good six minutes in and show them that I can play."

Even if that never happens, Ady can fall back on the thought that has helped him make a successful transition from Canada to Utah—he wouldn't change a thing.

He's found a home in Provo. He has friends to go out to eat with or to a dance after a game, not to a party with and get drunk. The struggles he had academically in Canada are now a thing of the past.

In his first semester at Provo, he was on the honor roll with a 3.80 GPA.

And in 10 years from now when he's playing basketball in a gym in Canada and someone says, "Hey, you're pretty good. Where did you play high school ball?"

Ady can then proudly point to his shirt "Provo Basketball" and say "Utah."

Undoubtedly, there will be a follow-up question. "What was it like to play basketball in the states? Was it tough? Was it worth it?"

He can truthfully say, "More than you will know."

CHAPTER SIX

THE RUN FOR NO. 1

News travels fast when it comes to Timpview. Just minutes after Provo polished off Pleasant Grove, Drury tells his team in the locker room there is a new No. 1 team in Utah.

Guess who?

You.

"Next week you will be ranked No. 1, because Timpview lost tonight."

The players look at each other with a bit of amazement—surprised that Timpview lost and excited about being No. 1.

In December, being No. 1 is cool. It's a position to aspire to; it's something to argue about and make a case for, but as the months pass by, the novelty wears off. No one wants to go into the state tournament ranked No. 1. No one wants that pressure.

But for now, Provo will take it. The Bulldogs have been ranked second behind Timpview all year. Now on January 3, there will be a changing of the guard.

With the Hawaii trip in the rearview mirror, Provo must now focus on running the table in non-region play. Its first challenge will be to play at Davis, the defending 5A champions.

If you could point to Provo's schedule and predict a letdown, the game at Davis would be it. The Bulldogs have been off for a week since they returned from Hawaii. Now the challenge is getting the team to focus on basketball again.

Drury stands at center court while coach Keli and Schooney run different drills on each end of the court. As usual, Schoonover has the guards, and coach Keli has the post players. Drury checks his palm pilot and says, "This is my favorite time of practice. I can let the coaches do their thing."

"Work on back-pick alley-oop," Drury says. Then he tells sophomore Tyler Miller he's catching the ball too low and tells Pututau, "There's no way in the world you can make that pass from your hip." Drury takes over and shows the guards how it's done. He makes two decent passes, but the third one is perfect, it's even a look-away pass to Stringham for an alley-oop dunk.

Provo then turns its attention to work full-court pressure. Drury calls it "51." It's effective—nine out of 10 times, it leads to a turnover.

Drury notices one problem with the defense. Cory Carter isn't doing it right. "Hands up, Cory. Hands up, we want him to throw that bounce pass. If he throws the bounce pass, it's slow."

When Provo goes to five-on-five, it's time to see if the full-court press will work. Immediately Drury notices Carter hasn't caught the vision, so he lines up on Kenyon Koop straight up.

"Which way are you sending him?" Drury asks. He points to the middle.

"How are they (his teammates) going to know that? You're straight up on him. He may not be able to beat you, but I guarantee there's guards in this state that would rip your butt off." (Drury goes around Carter on the outside and starts dribbling up court).

Frustrated by the team's ineffectiveness on the press, Drury turns to Schooney and says, "Coach, I'm about ready to throw this out (51). They're just being stupid. We should have been out of this drill 15 minutes ago. We've taught you this four times."

The players then respond. Hagen comes up with a steal and a layup. Drury shouts, "Good, we'll take that. Yes."

Satisfied with the drill, Drury gets out his palm pilot again and feels it's safe to move onto something else. Now it's time to work on an alley-oop play to Stringham. Since other teams have picked up on the fact that Stringham isn't a scorer, they have sagged off of him on defense. So Drury will counter with an alley-oop play that should keep teams more honest. If the alley-oop play breaks down, the second option isn't a bad one either. Hagen, who sets a pick, will be open for a three-pointer.

"You (Stringham) can't make that a turnover (the alley-oop pass). We played Mountain View and they had a guy who could really get up. They ran that three times early and how many times did they score on it?"

Drury holds up his hand—zero.

"It ended up being three extra possessions for us. It may have looked good, but it was a turnover," Drury adds.

A few minutes later, the team runs the alley-oop play to Corbin, who is 5'-10", which gets a good laugh from everyone.

Ready or not, Provo now takes aim at Davis.

Davis may not have the top talent in 5A, but it's a school rich in tradition. The school opened in 1914 and the current gym the team plays in was finished in 1958, but it will be phased out next year with a newer model.

Davis won its first state championship in 1920 and has won seven state titles overall. Only four schools have won more state titles than Davis, and for the last 13 years the program has been in good hands with Jay Welk. But the Darts are having trouble defending their 5A title. They got off to a 1-6 start, but four of those losses were by three points or less and Drury knows any win at Davis, no matter how down the Darts are, is a big win.

From the opening tip, Davis takes control of the game. The Darts jump out to a 9-2 lead at the end of the first quarter thanks to a patient offense that limits Provo to five first-quarter shots. Provo's only basket is a Tai Wesley bucket inside.

Drury doesn't panic, nor does he rip his team. He's very calm and collected when he says, "We've run two plays and we ran both of them wrong."

Welk is hoping Davis' deliberate offense will frustrate Provo into taking quick shots and shoot themselves out of their game plan.

But it doesn't work. In the second quarter, the Bulldogs turn the game around. Tika scores inside, then pulls down an offensive rebound and scores again.

Hagen then makes the play of the game. He zips down the lane where he appears destined for a head-on collision with a Davis player. But he steers to the left and does a double-pump windmill shot around another Davis defender that goes in. Provo trails by just one at 9-8.

Meanwhile, Provo's defense tightens its grip on a patient Davis team that seems intent on taking a good shot even if it takes a minute for each possession.

A Rand Sargent free throw gives Davis its first points of the second quarter at the 4:32 mark. With 1:50 left in the half, Pututau hits a three-pointer from the corner that gives Provo its first lead of the game at 11-10. The half ends with a basket from Davis' Jace Welk and an inside bucket from Craig Stringham that makes the score Provo 13, Davis 12.

Drury is pleased with the second quarter, but is alarmed at the execution of the offense.

"We scored 11 second-quarter points on at most, eight offensive possessions. That's a pretty good percentage. What I'm disappointed with the most is your execution. You've got to come to the party. Bench, the bench is shortened. Sorry guys, but I can't afford to play more than the six guys who have played in the first half when the tempo of the game is like this. If the tempo picks up, that may change."

There's one more thing to say before the team takes the floor again. "If you want to win, you'll win," Drury says.

Tai opens the second half by sinking a pair of free throws. After a Davis turnover, Provo tries to run a play called "Utah," but it doesn't work, so the Bulldogs settle for a Stringham 12-foot jumper.

After Sargent scores for Davis, Provo runs "Schoonover," which produces a Hagen three-point attempt on the wing. This time the play is run right, but Hagen's three-pointer is off the mark.

When Davis commits another turnover, Drury tries again. He yells out "10," but it doesn't work either.

Fortunately, Provo's defense gives the Bulldogs another shot. Pututau hits a short jumper and Stringham hits four free throws. Hagen added four points to help the Bulldogs open up some breathing room at 27-20 by the end of the third quarter.

The Wesleys then lead Provo to its biggest lead of the game when they combined on a 7-0 run to give Provo a 34-20 lead with 6:15 left in the game.

Davis has one more run left in it. Jace Welk hits a three-pointer to cut the lead to 36-30 with 2:10 left in the game. Pututau then missed a layup, but Tika hits a layup and Tai scores six points, including four free throws down the stretch to help Provo hold on for a 44-33 win.

"You closed it out beautifully," Drury tells his team in the locker room. "I'm very happy with the game, but I'm disappointed in the execution of the plays. Davis taught us some lessons in execution. You can't go out and execute one out of four plays. We probably ran 15 plays didn't we Mick? I'd say we only executed on three or four plays. We've got to do better than that. Let's take a minute."

The players are all on the bus and they're ready to sing, but Drury tells them to wait until they leave the Davis parking lot, out of respect. So as soon as the bus leaves the parking lot, the players slide down the windows and sing for all their worth.

"Oh, I'm a Bulldog, I'm a Bulldog, I'm a Bulldog from Provo High. I'd rather be a Bulldog than a ?$#%& from Davis High."

Now just what is said varies from person to person and from game to game. When Mercer is asked what is said, he described it this way. "Everyone says their own thing, but let me just say this. It's not good."

Suddenly, the bus radio is turned off and Mercer has the stage.

"Ok, I'd like to give out our nominations for the Scrub Cup," Mercer says as the bus erupts with a roar. Players pound on the top of the bus and beat on the top of the seats with their hands like they're in the middle of a drum solo.

Cory Carter's not here (he went home with his parents), but he's nominated for an air ball on a three-pointer.

Cheers fill the bus.

Joey, for missing that two-foot shot.

More cheers.

Tai for smacking that kid (a Davis player).

Steve (Torkildson) for throwing up a wild shot with 10 seconds left in the game.

The winner is Craig, for knocking over one of their cheerleaders (while chasing down a loose ball).

Speech. Speech.

"I'd like to thank you for this award. This is my second one of the season. What can I say, she was hot."

With that said, the team begins to sing again like someone just put five dollars in the juke box.

A big road win at Davis is a big step forward. Now the Bulldogs must face the surprise team of Region 7, Pleasant Grove.

※※※

In years past, Pleasant Grove has been in the same region as Provo. Thankfully for the Vikings, Provo is in a different region, but the Bulldogs are still on their schedule.

Schoonover is a Pleasant Grove alumni, but he didn't win a region title at Pleasant Grove when he was there (he graduated in 1993) and the Vikings haven't won one since. Many of the best players in the school's boundaries transfer to other schools, leaving Pleasant Grove at a disadvantage.

But this year's team is proving to have some promise. Coach Randy McAllister, in his first year, has the Vikings off to a fast start that included an upset win over Box Elder to open the season.

Provo doesn't know much about Pleasant Grove. The coaches have only seen the Vikings play once, but it's enough to know who they need to stop. Todd Thurgood and Landon Hallman are the scorers to watch.

They also pick up on a strange play, but there is some debate on what it's called. The best guess is scissors.

Drury draws it up on the white board. "This guy falls out of bounds and throws it to Hallman in the corner."

Mick wonders how they get the pass by the backboard.

Drury says the pass goes under it.

Provo has little trouble with Pleasant Grove. The Bulldogs take a 14-10 lead after the first quarter and a pair of three pointers from Hagen and Pututau, along with a three-point play from Tika help Provo to a 27-16 lead at the half.

In the third quarter, the Vikings run scissors and Tika intercepts the pass. Later in the quarter Tai and Stringham get into foul trouble, so Drury points to Torkildson, who quickly checks into the game and quickly checks out. His shorts are on backwards and he's having trouble keeping them up.

Garrett Groesbeck checks in for Torkildson and makes the most of his minutes. He pulls down a pair of offensive rebounds and scores in the final minute of the third quarter to help Provo to a 39-26 lead.

Pututau then scores five quick points to start the fourth quarter to put Pleasant Grove away and help the Bulldogs to a 58-37 win.

Pututau led Provo with 15 points. Tai had 12 and Tika scored 11 points to go along with nine rebounds. Hagen struggled from the field. He scored just three points.

Drury asks him what time he will be in the gym to work on his shooting. "Eight," Hagen says.

"Then you better be there by six," Drury says.

In the team room after the game, Drury writes on the board. POG (Player of the Game)—Groesbeck.

Groesbeck scored four points and was a spark and not a liability during his few minutes of playing time.

"When I die and go to either heaven or hell, the longer I coach I guess I get closer to hell, I want to be judged based on my potential and how much I used it. Tonight Garrett played to his potential."

There is a Scrub Cup changing of the guard. Mercer is playing too much, so the mantle is passed to junior guard Jordan Snarr. There are a few requirements to be captain of the Scrub Cup. First, you need to be vocal and take charge. You have to find a cup (usually in the garbage can) to hand out as a trophy, and it's best if you never play so that you can concentrate on your job, keeping track of nominees. Snarr turns out to be the perfect man for the job. He keeps a white piece of paper and a pencil hidden behind him on the bench so he can take notes throughout the game.

He feels it's an honor. In his first game as Scrub Cup captain, it's an easy choice.

Steve: His shorts were on backwards.

Speech, speech.

This is the easiest decision of the year. The shorts incident is too good to pass up.

"I'm kinda pissed off right now, but thanks for the honor," Torkildson says.

Short and to the point, not bad for his first speech of the year.

When the players show up for practice on Monday, there's something noticeably different. The players all show up with their shorts on backwards. Their black practice shorts that have Provo Hoops just above the left knee are now on the back. They do defensive slides and after they're done Drury has them switch the shorts back.

Torkildson says he noticed right away, but it wasn't until Drury has them switch their shorts back the right way before anything is said.

"You guys are jerks," Torkildson says with a laugh.

"You're never going to live that down," Drury says as he smiles. "We took you out because you were pulling up your pants every two steps."

After the laughter dies down, the focus turns to the next game against Lehi.

Drury has Kade Koop take off his shirt, and he simulates Lehi guard Drew Robinson. He also shows the team how Lehi forward Hunter Baumgartner makes a move on the baseline and where he gets the ball in the low post.

With practice over, Drury takes time to let the team know what they'll soon be dealing with.

"The next three ball games we'll see what we're made of. Lehi is going to have the Utah Jazz bear (the mascot) entertain the crowd. Their trumping this as one of their big games. The next time there's an adjustment (realignment) they will be in our division. They are bigger than we are right now. They have a new coach who has been one of the most successful in 2A history. He's making some things happen over there. Remember, they beat us by 20 in the summer.

"Then Friday we go up against one of the best shot blockers (Timpanogos center Mike) Weitzeil. Last year he had seven blocked shots against us.

"We're 8-0 and ranked No. 1 in the state. We can act like a rooster and do a little struttin', because we're 8-0. We've worked hard, but you have to remember how we got 8-0. We had to have a little luck. We had to play a perfect final 45 seconds against Mountain View. We scored two points in the first quarter against Davis and against Waimea, you stunk the place up. Beat Lehi tomorrow. Don't let Lehi be the rooster."

As Drury predicated, the Lehi game is the main event. Lehi has turned the game into the biggest one of the preseason.

Provo's starting lineup is announced as a small but vocal group of Provo supporters cheer with each name announced.

Then the lights go out and spotlights swirl around the gym. A capacity crowd gives it up. Lehi fans are wearing glow-in-the dark bracelets of all colors.

The PA announcer sounds like a seasoned veteran. Dreeew Robinson. Hunter Baumgartner. Kris Jeee-nkins. Troy Wardellllll. The starters are introduced and the lights come on. The Jazz bear drives onto the court on his Harley Davidson and revs the engine.

The game is underway.

Provo is unfazed by Lehi's hype and proceeds to play its best opening quarter of the year. Tai Wesley opens the game with a power move past his AAU teammate Hunter Baumgartner. Baumgartner gets even with a basket on the other end.

Pututau then gets hot. He hits from 15 feet, but Lehi keeps it close, and after Robinson hits a three-pointer, the Provo lead is 11-9, but the Bulldogs then pull away. Pututau and Hagen hit back-to-back threes. Pututau is feeling it. He hits another three and Hagen then drives down the lane and dishes off to Tika for a layup.

The quarter ends with a Tai Wesley miss and a Pututau offensive rebound that he kicks out to Hagen, who pops a three to give Provo a 25-13 lead.

Wow, the Bulldogs are hot. When Drury falls asleep at night, when he has a good dream, this is what it's like. An offensive that executes the plays he draws up and a group of players who are playing up to their potential.

"Don't be satisfied," Drury says at the end of the quarter. "Don't relax. As good as you've played, you're only up 12."

Drury then turns his attention to his post players and reminds them what he told them in yesterday's practice.

"Which way did he (Baumgartner) go? Which way did he go? Sometimes you don't believe me until it happens."

Stringham and the Wesleys nod their heads and look for something to wipe the sweat off their faces.

The second quarter is a draw and Provo takes a 33-21 into the locker room at halftime.

"I think we jumped on them offensively and let down on the defensive end. To really blow teams out you have to get it going on both ends," Drury says. "I believe we can get 17 points (in the second half). If we just lay down we can get 51 points. What's going to make the difference on winning this game is on the defensive end."

Provo opens the third quarter like it opened the game. Hagen hits for three. Pututau and Tika add buckets, while Baumgartner keeps the Pioneers in the game with a pair of hoops for Lehi.

After a Stringham steal, Drury calls out the play, "Schoonover." Hagen peels around a screen and knocks down another three-pointer to give Provo its biggest lead of the game at 43-25 with 4:54 left in the quarter.

Lehi coach Craig Gladwell has seen enough and calls a timeout.

His Pioneers battle back and turn the momentum back in their favor. When Provo tries for one shot at the end of the quarter, Jeff Christofferson picks Hagen's pocket and races in for a layup to cut the lead to 48-37.

The Lehi run hasn't angered Drury. "They had a great quarter. That was their quarter and they only beat us by one," he says holding up one finger.

But in the fourth quarter, Provo's ineptitude on defense surfaces.

Tika picks up his third foul and Tai gets into a pushing match with Alex Allred while trying to establish his post-up position.

The two continue to lean on each other with more intensity. Finally, Tai's emotions get the best of him and he's called for an elbow to the head of Allred.

Drury is furious and quickly subs in Carter.

"Wake up. What are you doing? Did you think they weren't going to call the elbow? For heaven's sake," Drury tells Tai on the bench.

Lehi continues its comeback. Alan Bailey pulls down an offensive rebound and scores. Tika fouls Allred, who scores on the play and is fouled. Allred adds the free throw to cut the lead to 51-44 with 4:22 left in the game.

Drew Robinson then hits two free throws and when he follows with a three-pointer from the corner with 45 seconds left in the game, Provo is in danger of blowing an 18-point second-half lead.

But then Lehi makes a costly mistake. The Pioneers foul Hagen and he sinks two free throws with 42 seconds left to give Provo a 57-53 lead.

Provo head coach Craig Drury gives instructions to his team during a timeout.

Robinson slashes inside and leaves a driving layup short, but Allred grabs the rebound and scores.

The Bulldogs quickly inbound the ball and play "keep away" as the clock ticks down. Lehi finally catches up with Hagen and fouls him with three seconds left. Lehi didn't want to foul Hagen, but the Pioneers had no choice.

Hagen sinks the first free throw to make it a three-point game. Lehi then calls timeout, but it doesn't faze Hagen, who calmly drops in the second free throw to put the game out of reach and give the Bulldogs a 59-55 win.

Whew! What a win.

But there was no celebrating inside the locker room. The pride of Provo, the one ingredient that's made Provo so successful—defense—was missing.

"I swore that I would come in and be positive, but I can't be positive," Drury says. "I was wrong when I said I didn't think they could get 30 points in the second half. They got 34. Did you come out and say we've got a big enough lead that they won't catch us? That's rude to the guys who work hard every day in practice."

No one was immune. "Joey, you take home the game films and watch them, don't you? I want you to take home this one and watch how cocky and arrogant you played on defense.

"I was very disappointed with the effort from our guard line.

"Let's all learn from Tai's foul. Your battle became personal, between you and him. You knew they were going to call it and when they did it took the ball away from us and gave them free throws. You can't do that—play personal games. You're too valuable. That's one reason why I can never like Allen Iverson. He doesn't care what happens as long as he gets his shots."

The scolding continues from Coach Keli.

"Those teams who are on the state championship banners, if they would have scored 59 points, they would have blown their opponent out. If you don't believe me, I'll give you the score books and we'll go through them. We fulfilled our role offensively, but on defense we stunk."

Outside the locker room the somber mood lightens. Matt Logan, an assistant coach at Salt Lake Community College, waits for Tika.

When he comes out of the locker room, Logan says, "We need to get you to make a commitment to this place." He points to the Salt Lake Community College logo on his jacket. Logan was Wesley's AAU coach and loves the way Tika works inside the post.

On the bus, the Bulldogs slide down the windows as the bus leaves the parking lot. "I'm a Bulldog, I'm a Bulldog, I'm a Bulldog from Provo High and I'd rather be a Bulldog than a @&!#!$$! from Lehi High."

The bus ride to Provo is a short one, just 15 minutes, so it's time to get right to the Scrub Cup.

Coach Keli for giving everyone on the bench high fives.

Hagen for getting his pocket picked not once but twice.

Hagen for shooting an air ball after he hadn't missed from outside.

What would a Scrub Cup be without a Stringham sighting?

Stringham is nominated again for running into Angela, one of the Provo cheerleaders while chasing down a loose ball.

Tai for his elbow incident.

The winner is Tai.

Speech. Speech.

Still miffed at the defensive effort, Coach Keli tells the team no singing. Not tonight. Instead the radio is turned on.

The next day at practice, Schooney is working on four corners while Drury watches from the bench. Two straight turnovers prompt a response. "You're too nice," he says. "I'd make them run for every turnover."

"We'd be running every time," Schooney responds.

"That's okay."

The next time the green team turned the ball over, they were running.

Frustrated by Provo's lack of execution, Drury gets white tape and puts two X's on the side of the court. Now there's no excuse for players not to know where they are to go on the press.

Practice is long. Three hours, the longest of the year. Finally, the players line up to shoot free throws. Ady has a chance to end practice with two free throws as the team crowds around the key and watches, but he misses the first free throw so everyone runs a half ladder. Eric Walker shoots next. Stringham says, "Just relax and shoot it." Walker misses the first and everyone runs.

Sophomore Tyler Miller shoots this time and he too misses the first shot.

"This is the worst you've shot free throws all year. The pressure's on two or three guys and it's a good pressure," Drury says with a slight laugh like he's enjoying it.

More running.

Jordan Snarr is up next. He leaves it short. "Ahhh," the team moans.

More ladders.

The number of misses at the free-throw line coincides with the number of ladders the team runs. Stringham's patience runs out.

"MAKE A FREE THROW!" Stringham shouts.

It's Hagen's turn. He shoots. Swish. Practice over. Time for Timpanogos.

※※※

One of the worries in playing a 5-7 Timpanogos team is 6'8" senior center Mike Weitzeil, who had a career-high of 11 blocked shots against Provo last year.

He's just the type of player that could neutralize Provo's inside game. Add junior guard Mac Nelson, who played significant varsity minutes as a freshman, and Timpanogos figures to be a team that could give Provo trouble.

Unlike their game against Davis where the Bulldogs scored just two first-quarter points, Provo jumps all over Timpanogos to outscore the Timberwolves 17-8. Hagen hits a pair of three-pointers, Tika has four points, Pututau three, and Tai scores off an offensive rebound. The balance dazes Timpanogos.

But once again Provo has a disastrous quarter. After scoring 17 points in the first eight minutes, the Bulldogs offense sputters and manages just two points in the second quarter. So at the half it's Provo 19, Timpanogos 18.

Provo's locker room during halftime isn't filled with any smiles, despite the lead.

"I would like to go over to the Timpanogos dressing room right now and yell at them," Drury says. "They're not treating us like we're special. That's not fair. I'm going to yell at their boys and tell them they're not being nice to us.

"Maybe I'll go talk to Timpview's coach, who's in the stands watching us and tell him (his team) to come to my practice and play defense exactly like we do in practice."

Drury continues. "I can't get after the inside players because they haven't had a chance to touch the ball. We have got to move the ball—teamwork, togetherness, ball movement. If you don't do that then you're going to score another two points in the quarter and you'll get blown out of here."

It takes Provo 2:35 to score its first basket (Hagen), but it takes Timpanogos even longer. When Murray Tucker answers for the Timberwolves, there is 4:30 left in the quarter.

Provo is doing a solid job on Mac Nelson, the team's leading scorer. He came into the game averaging 15.2 points per game. He has just five points at the half, but a Nelson free throw cuts the Provo led to 24-23, with 2:30 left in the third quarter.

Tai then takes over. He pulls down an offensive rebound and scores. After a Cory Carter steal, the Bulldogs go down low to Tai for another basket. After a Timpanogos miss, Tai grabs another offensive rebound, scores, and is fouled.

He makes the free throw to complete a personal 7-0 run that helps Provo to a 31-23 lead. Weitzeil ends the run with a bucket for Timpanogos, but Hagen counters with a three-pointer to end the quarter and give Provo a 34-25 lead.

A Pututau three-pointer, a three-point play, and a pair of Hagen free throws help give Provo a 48-35 win.

After the game, Drury saw the two officials outside Provo's locker room and took the opportunity to talk about the game.

The officials called four offensive fouls on Provo during the game. One in particular was near the top of the key after Stringham had set a screen.

Drury: For nine games, I've been teaching them and that hasn't been a foul and what I'm concerned about is tonight it was a foul.

Official: I can only call a foul when I see one, I can't be

responsible for what some other official calls.

Drury: I don't think I have a bad reputation, do I?

Official: No.

Drury: I asked you to come and talk to me and you wave me off, you poo-pooed me.

Official: I didn't feel like I was putting you off, that was not my intent.

Second Official: We know the coaches who we can listen to and those who we can't.

With the Timpanogos game in the win column, the focus now turns to its oldest rival.

"Can you feel the excitement? Can you feel the excitement when you walk down the halls? I do. This school is excited about this team. You can feel the rumbling. You're on the edge of being a really good basketball team. You haven't crossed it yet, and I don't know if you ever will. I believe in you and I want you to believe in yourself."

Drury isn't finished.

"You're going to beat some teams by just walking onto the court when they say, 'Oh crap, there's Provo.' When you do, that's a bonus. We'll take that, but that's not going to happen very often. Davis was probably one of the weakest teams we've played, but they weren't intimidated, were they? That's a good win. I don't care if they played sophomores, anytime you win at Davis it's a good win. Tuesday, Orem will be opening up their new gym against us. Doesn't it always seem like whoever we play, there is something big going on?"

Over the years, the Provo/Orem rivalry has changed, but there's nothing quite like a Provo/Orem game to relive some memories.

CHAPTER SEVEN

A RECORD-BREAKING RIVALRY

The Celtics/Lakers, Packers/Bears, Ali/Frazier, Louisville/Kentucky, BYU/Utah, Provo/Orem.

When talking top rivalries in sports, which one of the above doesn't belong?

Before you answer, ask yourself this question. When was the last time you saw a high school basketball game that did not involve LaBron James that was played at a college arena so the fans could be accommodated?

When is the last time you went to a high school basketball game and saw 14,500 fans?

Get ready for arguably the most historic and tradition-rich high school basketball rivalry in the nation.

Before you roll your eyes, consider this. How many times have you seen a future NBA center play an entire high school game with a broken bone in his foot? Or how many times do you see one team that has three athletes who will go on to play pro ball in three different sports?

And how many times have you seen two rivals play each other for the state championship in back-to-back years with both games decided by one point and with both games being decided by the final shot?

This is the Provo/Orem rivalry.

There are a few things you need to know about a typical Provo/Orem game. First, the games are almost always close, the two teams outdraw some NBA teams, and Provo usually wins. Provo has won 14 state championships, Orem has won none.

Orem is usually good, but when it comes to playing Provo it's usually not good enough.

In the 1960s, Provo had a 13-2 record against Orem. In the 70s, 80s and 90s, Provo continued to dominate. In Jim Spencer's 20-year career he lost to Orem just once, and in Drury's years as head coach he has only lost to Orem twice.

The two teams started playing each other in 1957 when Orem High opened. There have been many classic battles over the years, but for the sake of simplicity, let's just focus on two of the most amazing years in this historic rivalry.

The season is 1972-73 and the first game between the two rivals is played at the Smith Fieldhouse on the campus of Brigham Young University.

What's wrong with Provo High School?

Get real. This game is the main event. There's no way a high school gym anywhere is big enough, so the two teams found an arena that could accommodate the crowd.

Provo won the first meeting of the 1972-73 season in what would prove to be typical form—a 58-57 win.

The rematch was sold out, so the game was moved to the newly opened 23,000-seat Marriott Center on the BYU campus where a push was made to set a national attendance record for a regular season game.

The game drew 13,818 fans, and the result was another close Provo win. This time it was a 64-61 victory.

Provo secured the win when Kim Stewart grabbed a key rebound. Provo center Brett Vroman had just fouled out and Orem's Don Allphin was at the free-throw line shooting one-and-one. Allphin missed the free throw. Stewart pulled down the rebound and passed off to guard Veryl Law with 10 seconds left in the game. Law was fouled. He then hit one of two free throws to put the game out of reach.

But Orem would have another shot at Provo. The year ended with a third meeting between the two rivals at the University of Utah's Special Events Center in front of a record crowd of 14,500 fans—more than the BYU/Utah game drew and the biggest crowd of the year to attend a basketball game in Utah.

Once again they played for the 4A state championship. Provo had a 49-44 lead late in the fourth quarter, but Jay Cheesman, who led

Orem with 25 points, helped the Tigers close the gap. Gifford Nielsen spotted Dave Card all alone under the basket with 1:04 left in the game to give Provo a 55-52 lead.

There was a reason Card was all alone. He was not considered a scoring threat. Card played just over a minute in the entire game and his layup was the only shot attempt he took all night. Despite his brief appearance, Card still found time to make another big play.

After Card's basket, Cheesman answered with 42 seconds left to cut the lead to 55-54. Provo tried to stall and run out the clock, but Orem intercepted a Provo pass and now had a chance for the last shot.

After a timeout, the Tigers tried to execute the play coach Harry Anderson drew up during the timeout. The play was basically a high screen—a pick-and-roll with guard Steve Hodson and Cheesman. It was a play the Tigers ran with continued success in their second game against Provo and now with the title on the line, they went back to their bread and butter.

But this time Provo was ready for it.

"We'd run the play before with success. I got dribble penetration and was successful in getting to the basket," Hodson explained. "They did a great job hedging the screen. I stepped back and was open from 20 feet out, but that's not the shot we wanted. I took a step forward, but by then they had recovered. Orem alumni would like to think I was fouled and Provo would say I wasn't. The reality was I wasn't fouled. They had such good size and I was a 5'-9" point guard, who was the second option on the play."

Hodson had no choice but to shoot. Time was running out. Card partially deflected Hodson's shot. Provo's Kory Sorensen came down with the loose ball helping the Bulldogs hold on to a thrilling 55-54 win.

"We had one last hope and that was for me to throw the ball through the hoop," Hodson said. "I had run out of room to maneuver, so that's what I did. I threw the ball and missed it."

The Bulldogs had done it again. Nielsen led Provo with 21 points. Brett Vroman added 18, and Vance Law chipped in with six points.

Provo finished the season undefeated at 24-0. Orem finished the year with a 21-3 record. All three losses were to Provo.

Nielsen, who led the team in scoring with a 19.6 point per game average, summed the game up best when he was asked what the turning point of the game was. He said, "The buzzer."

Both Provo and Orem returned a solid cast of players for the 1973-74 season, which set up three more classic games.

In the first game of the season, Provo jumped all over Orem for a 14-3 lead and a 32-14 bulge at the half, but Orem held Provo to just 10 second-half points and nearly pulled off an incredible comeback.

The Tigers had their chances. Provo hit just 7 of 13 free throws and missed the front end of four one-and-ones and also missed a pair of technicals on Vroman, one for dunking the ball.

But in the end, Provo held on for a 42-39 in front of 7,129 fans in the Marriott Center.

The Provo/Orem rivalry was at its peak. The two cities that bordered each other were sometimes impossible to separate. For instance, Provo coach Jim Spencer lived in Orem and his wife taught at Orem High School. During one game, the mayors of both Provo and Orem had a free-throw shooting contest at half time. That event was followed by a free-throw shooting contest between the editors of the Orem Geneva Times and the Provo Daily Herald.

Provo beat Orem 56-47 in the second meeting of the year. Vroman led the Bulldogs with 18 points and 16 rebounds, Mark Bowman had 16, Mark Jarman 12, and Vance Law scored 10 points in front of 10,629 fans in the Marriott Center. Orem's Robert Louder led the Tigers with 18 points, but it wasn't enough to keep Provo from extending its winning streak to 46 straight games.

The Bulldogs led by eight at the end of the first quarter and by as much as 12 in the first half. Orem got within a basket twice in the second half, but could get no closer.

"Those were really some of the most pressure-packed games I've ever been involved with, from the professional leagues on down," Vance Law said. "Every game was close. You just never knew which way it was going to go. It was the NBA finals wrapped up in one game."

The 1973-74 season ended in classic style, with a 43-42 win over Orem in the state championship game, extending Provo's winning streak to 52 games.

Orem led by six at the half, but could never pull away. The game was tied seven times in the first three quarters.

Orem trailed by one point with 31 seconds left. Coach Harry Anderson called timeout to set up a play, but the Tigers never got to run it. Vance Law stole the ball, but in a dramatic turnabout, Provo turned the ball over on a double-dribble call with 15 seconds left.

Much like 1973's state championship game, Orem had the last shot. This time Todd Williams took the final shot with four seconds left, with Brett Vroman and forward Robert Bowen in his face. The shot bounced off the rim, leaving Provo state champs again.

"That was some kind of ending," said Provo coach Jim Spencer. "I can't believe it. We were just too darned conservative. I guess we just wanted to give everybody a thrill."

This is how the *Orem Geneva Times* reported the last shot.

"To add to the likeness of last year's championship, it was Orem's 5'9" guard Todd Williams who attempted the last shot with four seconds remaining in the game over the outstretched arms of Brett Vroman and forward Robert Bowen, both of whom fouled Williams but the referees failed to call it."

Vroman led the Bulldogs with 21 points and played the entire game with a broken bone in his right foot. In Provo's semifinal win over Highland, Vroman suffered a stress fracture in the first half. He played the entire second half of the Highland game in pain. In the finals, Vroman received a pain killer injection to help him deal with the injury.

Louder led the disappointed Tigers with 13 points and the 10,500 fans in attendance had just seen a state championship game and the peak of a rivalry that would never be matched again.

"It's pretty incredible that two teams a mile apart would have three professional athletes on the floor. I don't think that's ever been seen in Utah," Hodson said. "When I played at Southern Utah we played a game and they told me the place would be packed with 2,500 fans. They asked if I was going to be nervous. I just laughed. I played in front of 15,000 fans in high school."

Louder has similar memories of the old rivalry.

"Those were the glory days of high school basketball," Louder said. "I have a lot of bitter-sweet memories. Back then it was such a big deal between the communities. It was an exciting time to be a player."

Louder returned to coach at Orem for five years where he never did beat Provo as a coach either. He now coaches the girls team at Timpanogos High School.

As the Utah County area grew, the rivalry diminished, and when Timpview was created in 1977, Provo had a new rivalry. Orem had to take a back seat.

So when Orem wanted to open its new gym, guess who the Tigers played?

On January 13, Orem hosted No. 1 ranked Provo.

The junior varsity game was held in the old historic gym, while the girls varsity team played in the new gym with the boys varsity game to follow.

During the JV game, Drury leaned back on the benches in Orem's historic gym and watched the JV team pull off a stunning last second-shot. With one second left in the game, the Bulldogs had to inbounds the ball and get off a shot all in one second.

It would take perfect execution, unlikely at any level of basketball. Jordan Snarr inbounded the ball from the side. He threw a perfect lob pass to Dustin Migliaccio, who caught the ball just outside the key and shot all in one motion. Migliaccio fell to the ground and watched his shot go in, sending the game into overtime.

While Orem's JV team pulled ahead, Drury expressed his pregame thoughts.

"I'm hollow. I'm so nervous. They (Orem) could come out and lay an egg or they could score 50 points in the first quarter on us. I know they're going to be sky high."

When asked if he subscribes to the theory of it being good to lose a game before heading into the state tournament, Drury says, "Theories are only something newspaper guys subscribe to. Now if we lose tonight I'm going to come out and lie and say yeah, we needed to lose to get us more focused, but I don't believe in that. I go into every game as a coach wanting to win."

A loss might be good in the long run, but not tonight. Not at Orem. Not on this night. A Provo win over Orem is a good thing in any season at any time and in any event.

Orem was originally going to open the gym against Timpview, but it wasn't ready and figured opening against Provo would be fitting to appease the old timers.

Mike Conner, Orem's coach, had high praise for Provo. "They have great chemistry and role definition. If I had to pick now, I'd take them even though I think Timpview has the most talent."

Drury has only lost to Orem twice since he's been head coach. He figured his record against Orem is something like 24-2. Jim Spencer only lost to Orem once and Dolan Condie says he only lost to Orem once.

In the locker room before the game, Drury says, "Let's have some fun. Very few high school kids get the chance to open a new gym. We appreciate them opening the new gym for us. Now let's go give them a show."

Provo gets off to one of its patented slow starts. A Brooks Christiansen steal and basket gives Orem a 7-6 lead at the end of the first quarter.

But the second quarter is all Provo. Hagen opens the quarter with a three-pointer. Tika and Tai then combine to score the next 10 points as Provo opens the quarter on a 13-1 run.

The Tigers don't get their first points of the quarter until Christiansen hits one of two free throws with 1:38 left in the half.

Orem comes back to close the lead to 19-12 at the half after scoring the final four points of the half.

"They've been behind in every game at the half. I know their program. Right now they're over there getting in their face. They're going to emphasize getting more physical. They're expecting them to pick it up. They're going to try and beat you with conditioning and getting you to make mistakes. I don't think your shot selection has been bad, but we need ball movement. Aggressive ball movement."

Early in the third quarter Pututau sprains an ankle chasing down a pass from Hagen. Carter comes in for Pututau.

Orem's leading scorer Lincoln Reid opens the second half with a basket to cut the lead to 19-14, but Provo gets an unexpected boost from Carter, who hits a pair of three-pointers and Stringham, who decides to shoot after being left all alone.

Stringham, who averages just 4.0 points per game, erupts for seven points in the quarter, including a three-pointer at the buzzer to give Provo a 36-27 lead.

The game is effectively over when Hagen hits three straight three-pointers. After he hits the third one, he takes both fists and taps his headband three times.

He would get a Scrub Cup nomination for it. "I did it for good luck," he said with a rare smile. "Some might think it's kind of arrogant or that I'm being cocky, but I'm just having fun out there."

Hagen hit four 3-pointers on the night and finishes with 17 points, a season high. Tika has a quiet but impressive night with nine points, seven rebounds, and six assists. Tai has 13 points.

Provo opens up a big lead late in the fourth quarter and Drury calls a timeout to get his subs in the game. Ady has a breakaway layup, but is undecided whether to dunk or to lay it up and misses the layup, giving Corbin Mercer, who was there for the rebound, a chance to get in the box score.

The final score is Provo 58, Orem 39. Chalk up another win in the rivalry for Provo.

After the game an Orem fan congratulates Drury. "Your guys can play."

Drury admits, "We're okay. I like us."

There's mostly praise for accomplishing something Drury didn't think he'd see, a perfect preseason, an 11-0 start.

Schoonover says, "I divided the season into three parts. Preseason, Region, and State tournament. We're 11-0 in the first part of our season and it's because we've kept focused and played our roles. Corbin plays two minutes a game sometimes, but when he win he's happy.

"I've coached close to 500 games, and this is one I will remember with all the hoopla. You handled the hoopla just right. When you play right, gosh you're good, but when we play down, we're just mediocre."

The only negative of the night is directed at Pututau, who has his ankle wrapped in ice and propped up on Hagen's knee.

"Maybe you don't understand what to do, but we're running plays for you and you're not getting it done," Drury said. "You're too valuable to us. I've never had three better pickers than I've had this year. Usually, guys don't like to set picks because they're afraid they'll get hurt.

"Craig gets a 10 for the way he's playing his role right now. He's doing it right. He's fun to watch right now. My wife says he's her favorite player to watch. Don't you guys make fun of him. She's a grandmother of 12, she can have her favorite player. Let's take a minute."

The Scrub Cup nominations are in: Mick is nominated twice, once for getting the ball stolen again and once for tapping his headband three times after hitting his third straight three-pointer.

Coach Corbitt for getting hit by the remote control car at halftime going into the locker room.

Stringham for getting angry after going after a loose ball and committing a hard foul.

The winner is Scott Ady for blowing a layup at the end of the game.

"I'm honored to have the Scrub Cup a second time. I'm down with the Scrub Cup. I don't think I deserved it. I missed a layup. Cory Carter got swatted huge in the game. I thought Cory Carter deserved it, but I'm always privileged to take it. I should have tried dunking it anyway. I wussed out."

When Hagen emerges from the locker room, there are two Orem girls who want a picture with him. He gives one of the girls his headband and poses for a picture with another girl. Drury stands behind Hagen and the girl and poses with a peace sign over their heads.

The bus leaves without Drury, who walks to his truck in the parking lot.

"Two years ago I had to yell at my team to get them to do anything. This group is different. Mick Hagen can be the best player in the state and the worst. If I yell at Mick, he'll go the other direction. Every person is different. With Mick I have to talk to him calmly."

The Bulldogs are on a roll and Drury is happy. These are the times where the size of a paycheck doesn't matter. It's nights like these that money can't buy.

Drury opens the door to his truck, then turns back to add a nightcap to the night.

"I just want to play. I wish we could play all of our games in the next 10 days."

CHAPTER EIGHT

THE CASTING OF ROLE PLAYERS

They have their sweats on while the game is being decided. They sit on the bench and cheer and hope…they hope that Drury will turn to them and point.

"You're in."

And when they get in the game, they are the "X" that sets a pick for the shooter. Or they are the fifth option in case everything else breaks down.

On the bench you find players who work just as hard, and in many cases harder, than those whose names are introduced as the starters.

They don't know how many shots they will get per game, if any. They don't know how many minutes they will play each game, if any. But still they show up to practice every day and hope someday their role will change. Maybe someone will get hurt. Maybe they'll get hot and hit every shot they take. Maybe they'll play so well that coach won't be able to take them out of the game. Maybe someone will get in foul trouble.

They are optimistic. They speak in terms of the future and their vocabulary always includes "maybe."

They are the role players of the team and how well they play their parts can make or break a season.

When people talk about team chemistry, they're talking about the players on the bench. Can they accept a lesser role? Can they still play their role knowing their names are never going to show up in the newspaper and no one at school will ever be talking about a shot they took during the game.

Can they rehearse their lines day after day knowing they may never get a speaking part?

It's much easier to be a role player when you are a sophomore or a junior because there is the belief that next year will be different, but when you are a senior, it can become the biggest test of their athletic lives.

There are three role players who are seniors on this year's team. They would have loved to try out for the lead role, but ended up being typecast as character actors, and all three faced different challenges.

Corbin Mercer, Craig Stringham, and Steve Torkildson share a bond as role players. Mercer and Torkildson would often joke around that if they transferred to a smaller school, they would be stars.

In truth, Mercer and Torkildson wouldn't have to go to a 1A school to change their part. There are plenty of teams in 4A that would love to have them, teams where they could score in double figures, or teams where they would be introduced as a starter, but at Provo their need to be the star takes a back seat to their desire to win.

Stringham starts, but he doesn't score. Mercer and Torkildson don't play. But their approach to the game, their patience when it comes to playing time, is admirable.

Role players are not used to having reporters talking to them. They seem surprised that anyone would be interested in them, but they are in many ways the most interesting. What they have to say is often the most revealing.

Every team has players like Stringham, Mercer and Torkildson. Will they complain behind the locker room door about the coach? Will they stir up their teammates to play for their own agenda? Will they spend their senior year in misery destroyed by the belief that they deserve better, that they are victims of the politics of coaching?

If they are bitter, they're not saying so. To those who know them best, this is no surprise.

Mercer is 5'-10" guard who has dark brown hair and bushy eyebrows and has a competitive streak in him that exceeds his level of talent. He usually looks serious and when it comes to improving his game, never forgets to punch the time clock. When it comes to basketball Mercer is good at most things—ball handling, shooting, passing and defense—but he's not great at any of them and in a program like Provo's, that often gets you relegated to a backup.

He's not as talented as Hagen, who has been a three-year starter,

Provo coach Craig Drury gives some instruction to guard Corbin Mercer.

and he's not as good of a shooter as Carter, who has proven to be instant offense off the bench.

So where does that leave Mercer?

Fighting for minutes. Any minutes.

When Drury was asked about Mercer, he said, "He's been coming off the bench as a senior. He's handled it better than any kid we've ever had, yet he's been a leader. He was able to lead by example. He's worked harder than anyone else in practice."

The Mercer family has been around Provo high since the 1940s. Corbin's grandfather Don Phillips played on the 1941 state championship team for Provo. His older brother Glade graduated in 1999 and was part of two state championship teams at Provo (1997, 1998).

Glade came off a knee injury in the fall of his junior year that held him back. As a senior he came off the bench behind Mick's older brother Brad.

Glade was six feet tall, which is what Corbin is listed at in the team's program, but that's nothing more than a favor to Mercer. When cornered on the subject he says he's really 5'10" and 145 pounds.

Despite his stature, there is something about Mercer—a guy who's got one part talent, two parts heart, and three parts competitiveness—that would give him a spot on any team. He is a role model of work ethic. His teammates call him "Little Fury," which is as good as any way to describe him.

Corbin watched Provo win a state championship in 1995 when he was in elementary school. After watching Provo win it all, he was hooked. He didn't miss another Provo home game.

"In offseason he would line up all of our games. Coach would say, 'Corbin get a team here to play at this time.' He would get the keys to the gym for open gym," Schooney said. "He knew Mick was going to play, but he never did complain to me. He didn't want to hurt the team."

It seems as though everyone likes Corbin. He's dated the same girl for more than two years. He's fiery, but also sensitive. He cried during the last episode of the tv show *American Idol*.

"I love him. He's like a bulldog. Even though he's so little, he's tough. No one works harder than he does," said assistant coach Cory

Green. "When he gets in the game even if it's for two minutes, he gives you everything he has. Coach has to find him more minutes."

Stringham is a 6'5" tall and lanky blonde with long side burns and who walks like he is leaning slightly backwards. The stats girls, Valerie and Laura, laugh when Stringham walks by.

"He definitely walks with a strut," they say in unison.

Stringham loves Mexican food, but he'll eat just about anything. One time he ate a 24-inch sub in 15 minutes.

Other than basketball, he loves to play baseball. He is one of the team's top pitchers and, if you talk too much or irritate his teammates, you could expect to get a fastball in your ribs. He admits he's thrown at people who had it coming.

Stringham is the team's free spirit. He is an Oakland Raiders fan. He'd fit right in with his face painted silver and a patch over his eye. He often answers dates for other people.

The days of simply saying yes or no to a dance are long gone, out with the shag carpet and the bellbottoms.

Now days you have to get creative when you say yes. What could be more creative than having Stringham show up on the doorstep with a guitar and very little on, then work the word "yes" into his song for one of his friends?

He is the team's entertainment. On bus rides home, it's common to hear, "Go Craig, go Craig, go Craig," as he does a striptease with his shorts.

Off the court, he goes by Stringham standard time.

"He doesn't care," Mercer said. "If he's supposed to pick up his prom date at 8 p.m., he'll show up at 8:30 p.m. He doesn't care."

He also doesn't care if he scores. A successful game for Stringham is if he gets in double figures in picks set, not points scored. He will grab a rebound, he will throw an elbow, he will do whatever it takes to win, and that is just a description of the way he practices. His knees are red and usually have scabs from floor burns.

As a freshman, Stringham scored 25 points, what would prove to be a career high. He was the team's go-to guy when he was on the sophomore team, and as a junior he often scored in double figures on the junior varsity team, but as a senior all that has changed.

After one game, one of his friends said, "Hey Craig, nice game, you scored eight points."

"Oh, really? I didn't think I had that many."

Just because he's not an offensive threat doesn't mean he's not competitive. No one on the team is more competitive. He could have made an impact on the football team but opted not to play.

Why not?

"They lose too much," he said.

"I just want to win a state championship," Stringham added. "That's the only thing that matters to me."

The Stringham name has been around Provo for more than a decade. Matt Stringham started it, but he didn't play basketball; he opted for football and baseball. He is 11 years older than Craig. Jed, who is nine years older than Craig, played basketball and baseball and went on to play baseball for the University of Utah. Then there's Breeze, who is three years older than Craig. He played football and baseball for Provo.

Now there's Craig. The youngest of five kids, the last in line. Not everyone has such a support group.Soon those hectic days will be missed. The Stringham family will be longing for the old days.

Steve Torkildson has never been in one place long enough to develop a support group. His mother, his brothers and sisters were in North Dakota and his father was in Thailand when Provo started its season.

Torkildson was born in Stanley, North Dakota, but the family bounced around from one place to another. Call it a hazard of the profession. His father was a circus clown for 15 years, which was no laughing matter since his parents divorced when Torkildson was eleven. His father took off and could hardly support himself, never mind eight children and an ex-wife.

Steve has an older brother and one older sister, but he still spent much of his time caring for his brothers and sisters, which made it all the more difficult to overcome the tragedy that stung the family.

When Steve was 12 he was sick for about two weeks. He's not sure what he came down with, the best guess was the flu, but he would never know because his mother wasn't big on going to a doctor. Eventually Steve got better, but about the same time he recovered, his brother (four years younger) got sick.

The family figured whatever Steve had was going around, but that all changed the morning that Steve woke up and found his brother on the floor—dead.

"He wasn't breathing," Steve said. "We thought he had the flu, but what we didn't realize was he had diabetes. It was tough because I was really close to him."

Eventually Steve was able to cope with the shock of his brother's death, but it took time. By his own admission, he didn't have any friends. He was a product of home schooling and never got involved in sports. By the time he attended public schools he was in eighth grade and then it wasn't a basketball that he carried around, it was a trumpet.

He began playing the trumpet and was no slouch. Thanks to the financial support of his grandmother, each summer Steve attended band camps across the country, including Canada where he was often first chair.

But as a ninth grader, Steve began to show interest in basketball. He had always been bigger than other kids his age. Even though he didn't know the rules, it didn't matter. He was 6'7" and coaches always have more patience with big guys.

After just two years of playing the game, he showed enough promise to make Provo's team and was encouraged when Drury told him he had natural ability.

But it seemed like nothing ever came easy for Torkildson. There was trouble at home. His mother wanted to move again. Over the years, Steve has lost count of how many times his family has moved. He estimates he's lived in 15 different states and has moved 30 times. But that's a guess. He quit counting.

Steve was tired of moving and now that he had a promising basketball career that he didn't want to interrupt, he finally resisted. Enough already. He had put down his anchor.

When his mother and his brothers and sisters moved back to North Dakota, Steve wasn't with them. Instead he struck a deal to stay with his aunt.

It allowed him to stay in Provo, but his aunt didn't have the means to support him. There was little money for food and none for other needs in life, so Steve stole what he needed. He seemed justified at first; a guy has to eat. But the more he took, the easier it got. Then he got caught and was arrested.

"It was really stupid. I realized after I got caught, that wasn't me. I did a lot of praying. It made me a better person," he explained.

Drury now had a decision to make. Should he keep Torkildson on the team? Or would it be better to cut him for fear he would be a trouble maker?

If anything were to happen to Tika Wesley or even Tai, he could use Torkildson, but it didn't look like he was going to start ahead of either one of them.

Steve's mother wanted him to move back to North Dakota, but Drury knew Steve needed basketball and actually lobbied for him to stay in Provo instead of moving again.

Steve got his way. He stayed and it turned out to be the biggest move of his life. If it weren't for basketball, Torkildson admits, the motivation to change wouldn't have been so compelling. If it weren't for basketball, who knows where he would be—what he would be doing. He shudders to even think about it.

Torkildson moved in with a friend's family and life began to change. His friends on the basketball team were now his support group. His coaches gave him the discipline he needed and in the fall of his senior year just before basketball began, he went to the Provo/Timpview football game and met a cheerleader named Jackie.

Steve wasn't exactly Mr. Outgoing, so of course he didn't say anything, but Jackie did.

"I'd seen him at school, but I'd never really talked to him," she said. "I just asked him if he wanted to hang out."

The two quickly became inseparable, and within a year, Steve's life had direction. There was a goal. He now had two reasons to stay out of trouble.

Steve concentrated on basketball and began to show promise. After an injury-filled junior year, as a senior there have been times in practice when he looked like he could be an all-state player during half-court scrimmages and shooting drills.

What he lacked more than anything else was confidence. What he lacked was playing time, but with Tika and Tai Wesley ahead of him, he wasn't likely to get many minutes.

Steve Torkildson goes up for a shot against Springville's Glen Young.

So Steve joined Corbin on the bench and even though neither one of them played as much as they wanted to, they never did look around to see if the grass was greener somewhere else. They are content with their roles. They are proud to be in Provo.

There are other team members who check in for spot duty. Their varsity minutes can be measured with a teaspoon and not a measuring cup, players like Kade Coop and Garrett Groesbeck, but they're not seniors. They have next year.

For Stringham, Mercer, and Torkildson there won't be a next year. They all faced their own unique challenges as role players and the reviews are in. They each received four stars for the way they handled it.

"I wouldn't want to play for anyone else," Mercer said. "I wish I had the opportunity to play more. I saw myself doing more. Me and Steve would always joke that if we moved to Emery (High School), we'd be all-staters."

So when the season is over, what does that say about Mercer,who didn't play a minute in the Mountain View game?

By the time Mercer was a senior, just when he thought it was his turn, that he'd paid his dues, someone else cut in line.

Was it easy?

What a stupid question. Little Fury never went through anything tougher in his athletic life. There were times when he wondered what he had done wrong. Times when he wondered if life would be different had he been at another school, but those were just fleeting thoughts. Those feelings may have been as hot as boiling water at one time, but he let them go, they evaporated.

What does that say about Mercer?

It says it all.

CHAPTER NINE

REGION WARS

On a subfreezing Thursday night in January, several crazy people are riding four-wheelers around a Provo neighborhood. Who in their right mind does that?

When the four wheelers pull over and the engines are turned off, their identities are revealed—it's Pututau, Hagen, Ady, and their dates.

Be advised, if one of these guys asks you out, it's not likely you're going to dinner and a movie. Now that's not to say these three can't be romantic. After they got off their four wheelers, they served up dinner under the stars and there was even a variety of menu options. They could choose from Lucky Charms or Frosted Flakes, and the location was on the roof of a church.

The occasion is the El Cheapo Dance. The idea is brilliant—spend as little as possible, be a tightwad.

The players have no problem playing the role. Here's a look at Hagen's bill for the night.

A pair of matching painter jump suits: $4.99

Box of cold cereal and milk: free, since he swiped it from his parents' house.

Admission to the dance: $5

Total coast of the date: $10

Payoff? Priceless.

Hagen picked up his date and drove her to his house. He then gave her a white painter jump suit to wear. The three couples climbed up on the roof of a church to enjoy their dinner and were nearly busted when a police car drove by, but that only added to the excitement of the night.

It looks like Hagen will meet the self-imposed deadline to have a girlfriend, and he'll do it two weeks before the February 1 deadline. The date went very well.

Go figure.

Hagen met his date after the Orem game. She's from Georgia and has only been in Utah for a few months. He's intrigued with her and doesn't want to mess around dating anyone else right now.

Ady takes Heidi, the same cheerleader that applied to be Hagen's girlfriend. The two stay over at Hagen's house talking until 2 a.m.

Pututau takes a girl in his neighborhood. His girlfriend's parents don't like the two going to every dance together, so for this dance, they each go with someone else.

Before the dance, Drury warned his players to call it an early night.

"This isn't a weekend," Drury said. "I suggest you leave the dance by 10 p.m. We've got Spanish Fork tomorrow. We'll have a shootaround at 11 a.m. and I don't want you out late. If I find out they you're out past 12, we'll be playing Spanish Fork without some of you."

Lobendahn threatens to check the dance to find out how late the players stay out.

There's no school the next day (teacher meetings) and no school on Monday (Martin Luther King Day), so the players disregard Drury's 10 p.m. suggestion. The shootaround isn't until 11, so they can sleep in and be fine.

Most of the team goes to the dance. Corbin went to Gandolfo's Deli for dinner with his long-time girlfriend.

El Cheapo is the prefect dance for Torkildson, who loses $50 to a sportswriter after he makes a fluke one-handed shot from the corner in front of the bleachers. He takes Jackie out to eat, and after the dance they go home to watch a movie.

Once the players are at the dance and having a good time, there's no way they're leaving at 10 p.m. Not one player leaves at 10 p.m. Most of the players get to bed between midnight and 2 a.m. Not exactly what Drury had in mind for pregame preparation, but there's something else for Drury to worry about besides his curfew—grades.

Friday not only marks the first day of region play, it's also the last day players can turn in work to raise their grades.

Provo School District policy allows players to have one "F" or one "NA" (no grade because of excessive tardies or absences). You can have one, but you can't have both. Despite the talk before the Lehi game (ten days earlier when Drury checked with each player one by one and asked him about grades), procrastination prevails and the players ignore Drury's warnings much like the dance curfew.

Dustin Migliaccio, Torkildson, and Ady all have NA's to make up for, but when the grades come out everyone is eligible. A disaster is avoided. Provo is at full strength for Spanish Fork, a team that has never beaten Drury.

When asked if he thinks the Dons are catching Provo at the right time, Spanish Fork coach Rex Brimhall takes the optimistic angle. "Sure, we're Spanish Fork. We're 3-7. I don't know of a better place to open region play than Provo."

After a pause and a smile, Brimhall adds, "It will be nice to get it over with."

The pregame talk in the locker room is brief.

"Don't try to figure things out. Just play," Drury says. "Play your triangles (referring to defense) and have fun. For heaven's sakes have fun out there."

Provo takes the court as PA announcer Saia Pope's music is rapping on the loudspeakers.

Who's house is this? It's the Bulldog house,
It's the Bulldog house.
Woof, woof, woof, woof,
Dawwwwg pound.
Woof, woof, woof, woof.

Tai Wesley scores five of Provo's first seven points of the game to help the Bulldogs jump out to a 7-2 lead. But Spanish Fork holds Provo scoreless for the final 4:45 of the first quarter and ties the game at seven.

Tai ends Provo's scoring drought with an offensive rebound basket with seven minutes left in the half to give Provo a 9-7 lead.

Provo's balance then helps the team break the game open. Hagen hits for three. Carter pops a three, Stringham and Pututau each add baskets and an offensive rebound putback from Tika Wesley gives

Provo a 21-11 lead at the half.

Provo forces seven second-quarter turnovers and gives up just four points in the second quarter.

"You're doing a super job on the defensive end and boarding the ball. You're killing the crap out of these guys and you're only up 10," Drury says in the locker room. "They are only three possessions away from you. They had shots that just didn't fall."

Spanish Fork cuts the lead to seven to end the third quarter, but midway through the fourth quarter, Hagen hits a jumper that gives the Bulldogs a 46-33 lead with just over four minutes to play and Provo fans begin chanting, "Hitch up the wagons," a reference to Spanish Fork's small-town reputation.

Provo finishes off Spanish Fork 54-39. The box score indicates Provo's scoring balance. Hagen leads the way with 14. Tai Wesley has 11, Tika and Pututau each finish with 10 points.

After the game, Drury wonders if the Wesleys have a brotherly rivalry going on.

"Do you like each other? When the ball comes down low, look for each other."

He then draws a box on the board and writes Timpview, American Fork, Payson and Provo in it. Outside the box is Spanish Fork and Springville.

"I'd rate these as the teams to beat in our region," Drury says. "Spanish Fork is trying to break in here and Springville, we've seen them once. They penetrate and kick. They have very little size, but they're very athletic. (Zac) Erekson is very athletic. Their team is not necessarily the best shooters, but at the same time they can shoot."

Nothing Drury says about Springville registers. The team has already made up their minds. They won't lose to Springville, they know Springville was embarrassed by Timpview 91-29 in its last game.

※※※

Three days later, Provo steps off the bus at Springville. The JV and sophomore teams arrive at 2:30, just in time to be greeted by the Springville students, who have just gotten out of school for the day.

As the last player steps off the bus, one of the Springville students yells, "Hey, try not to beat us by 60 like Timpview did."

Another student says, "Yeah, take it easy on us. At least let us score 30 points."

How do you keep from getting overconfident?

It wouldn't matter. Springville is one team the coaches have spent little time preparing for. They've scouted them just once.

Basketball at Springville High School has been a struggle with the exception of a few memorable seasons in the mid-1980s. In 1984, they reached the 3A championship game, only to lose to the Jordan High Beetdiggers. Then Springville had great seasons the following two years as future University of Utah and NFL quarterback Scott Mitchell played the low post, combining with all-state sharpshooter Les Chappell to lead the way.

But the winning seasons dried up again for several years until 1998, when Springville emerged as a 4A title contender behind the prowess of 6'4" guard Chad Jacobsen, who went on to play football at Utah.

Jacobsen averaged 31 points per game and helped the Red Devils to a 17-7 record and advance to the state championship game where they lost to Timpview.

Springville has been a basketball power in the past, winning a total of four state championships. The problem for Springville fans has been all four state championships were won before 1960, with the first coming before the Great Depression (1917), which is what basketball has been at Springville lately.

Since 1990, Springville has had four different coaches. The newest is Brent Knapp, who was an assistant coach in Idaho when he took the job.

Poor guy.

Springville's community is hard on coaches and not necessarily just basketball coaches.

One parent actually hired a private detective to dig up some dirt on a former baseball coach in an effort to get him fired. Stunned that anyone would go to such extremes, the coach resigned. There's not enough money in the entire school district to put up with that.

Springville High School made a name for itself around the state when a group tried to get some momentum going to get rid of the school mascot, the Red Devil.

The city was divided on the issue. Some parents didn't want to be cheering for the Devils, while others were angered at the thought of having to come up with a new mascot, just to be politically correct.

Springville voted the initiative down and the school hung onto its mascot.

When it comes to basketball, Springville's best athletes usually don't play or they transfer to another school, like Timpview. Matt Mortensen, a sophomore, who lives in Springville's boundaries, played his freshman year at Mountain View, but then transferred to Timpview this year as a sophomore.

Last year, Greg Smith resigned after Springville finished with a 3-17 overall record and didn't win a region game. In his eight years as head coach he had a winning record just three times, but it's widely accepted that Springville's talent level is usually at or near the bottom of the region.

This year, Springville had won just one game coming into region play and that came over Cedar City, a 3A team that finished with a 4-16 record.

The losses were bad enough, but Springville's region opener against second-ranked Timpview was a 91-29 embarrassment.

The lopsided score is greeted with shock and anticipation at Provo. The starters are shocked that Timpview won by so much and the reserves are excited about the opportunity of getting some serious playing time.

While the starters figured to play the game on cruise control and with very little emotion, the Springville game means a great deal to guys like Ady and Mercer, who are counting on this game to get some confidence back.

Even seldom-used junior Eric Walker, whose season high is one point, thinks he might even get some PT.

But Springville has heard the snickers around school and the team is determined not to be embarrassed like that again.

Provo jumps out to a 12-6 first-quarter lead, but Peter Monk hits a 23-foot three-pointer at the buzzer to make the score 12-9 at the end of the quarter.

As the second quarter continues, the confidence in Springville grows. When Munk pulls down an offensive rebound and scores, he is fouled. After converting the three-point play, Springville leads 23-22 with 2:39 left in the half.

This was shaping up to be the upset of the century.

But Provo begins to pull away, and when Hagen hits a three-point play, Provo is up 33-24, but the half is not over. Monk strikes again. This time Monk pulls up from 30 feet and sinks a three-pointer that beats the buzzer to cut the lead to 33-27 at the half.

"It doesn't matter how good or how bad you are if you play below your ability, then you have played down to their ability," Drury tells the team at the half. "They didn't think they could beat you. In the first quarter they were just hanging around. They were ready to roll over and die. All of the sudden we have five turnovers and now their locker room is like a football locker room. They're in there pumping their chests.

"We were very lethargic out there. Now we're only up six and we're in jeopardy of getting beat. We're not doing anything really bad, but we're not doing anything really right."

The third quarter starts out in a disastrous way. Tai picks up his fourth foul just 10 seconds into the quarter.

It takes Provo most of the quarter, but the Bulldogs finally begin to open a comfortable lead. Hagen hits a three and Tika powers inside for two to give Provo a 43-33 lead.

Springville comes back to cut the lead to 48-41 at the end of the third quarter, but the Bulldogs pull away again. A Stringham three-point play with 5:33 left gives Provo a 57-44 lead.

Kenyon Koop, a freshman, waits at the scorers table to check in with a minute left. But it doesn't look like he's going to get in. Finally, the ball goes out of bounds to stop the clock. Koop raises his fist in the air and turns to the bench and smiles.

There's 3.7 seconds left, but it doesn't matter. He got in.

After the game Drury reminds the subs this was their chance.

With Tai in foul trouble most of the game, Torkildson played in the second quarter and parts of the third and fourth quarter. He missed a jump hook in the second quarter and had the ball stolen from him in the third. The coaches blame it on concentration.

Jackie Boot, a senior cheerleader, looks on during a Provo game.

"Here's my advice," coach Keli says. "Tell the little lady (Jackie) to quit bothering you. I keep pushing for you really hard."

Drury interrupts, "I've turned him down."

"At some point if you don't produce, we'll have to put someone else in," coach Keli adds. "When I was in high school, I never had a girlfriend. Why would I worry about a girl when the surf's up?"

Drury cuts in. "Thanks coach. A 100 years ago, we had a guy name Jesse Clark. I told him I had a uniform, but he'd never play…"

Drury continues to tell the subs Clark's story of how he turned into one of the team's most valuable players, giving them hope if they continue to work hard that someday Drury will be telling players the story of Steve Torkildson.

When Torkildson got home he immediately called Jackie and said, "We need to talk. The coaches think you're distracting me. We need to breakup until March 4 or forever," he said.

Stunned by the news, Jackie is reduced to tears.

"It will still be the same. I'll still flirt with you," Steve says in his best effort to do damage control.

The next two days the word is out that Jackie is available and the calls for dates start to come in, including another one from Torkildson, who caves in.

"Will you be my girlfriend again?"

Jackie reluctantly takes him back but warns him, if he does that to her again, they're done.

After Drury is done with his post game talk, the team boards the bus only to discover a shocking sight. The girls team is already on board and they are in the back of the bus.

The boys have traditions to celebrate. They don't like having to change their post-game party plans. Usually the girls take a different bus, but a scheduled mixup has left both teams on the same bus.

Girls or not, traditions must live on.

The windows are rolled down and the singing begins as soon as the bus is in motion.

"I'm a Bulldog, I'm a Bulldog, I'm a Bulldog from Provo High and I'd rather be a Bulldog than a @#$$#% from Springville High."

Second verse same as the first.

"I'm a Bulldog, I'm a Bulldog, I'm a Bulldog till I die, and I'd rather be a Bulldog than a @#$@$ from Springville High."

Shout outs begin.

"Let's hear it for Joey's air ball."

They pound on the ceiling of the bus, which prompts the bus driver to pick up his radio.

"You guys can't pound the ceiling anymore. I got in trouble. There were dents in the ceiling."

More shout outs.

Give it up for the Sweep. Get out the brooms, all three teams, sophomores, junior varsity and varsity teams won their games.

Now the singing continues.

"I'll make love to you . . . ."

It's amazing, from Laura and Valerie, the two stat girls, who are considered part of the team, to the freshman and sophomores, they all know the song word for word even though it was popular in the early 1990s.

Now the team wants some entertainment and when they want to be entertained there's only one guy they turn to.

"Go Craig, go Craig (Stringham)."

The team wants Stringham to strip down to his jock, but Stringham can't be persuaded with the girls team looking on.

Pututau says, "Give it up for stage fright."

Since Stringham won't offer the entertainment, the team picks on someone else. Corbin starts a new chant, "Go Schooney, go Schooney."

Schooney laughs and shakes his head.

Life is good.

The team is ranked No. 1 in the state. They are undefeated on the season and more importantly they are undefeated in region play.

There is still time to sing one more song before the bus pulls into the Provo High School parking lot.

"Do de dah do, do de dah do, ooh, I feel wonderful tonight."

CHAPTER TEN

TIMPVIEW

It's 9:30 a.m. and something is happening inside Provo High's gym. There's a series of cheers, followed by laughter.

What is going on? This doesn't sound like a P.E. class. There are no sounds of squeaking gym shoes or bouncing balls.

It's quickly obvious that if you're outside the gym, you're outside the epicenter. Each row in the gym is filled with Provo students, who are roaring their approval at two gladiators who are at center court. Two girls are wrestling on a plastic tarp covered with chocolate pudding.

Bravo!

The entertainment continues. Next a male student swallows a goldfish that's still wiggling. On another section of the court, a girl gets a sundae makeover, complete with several scoops of ice cream that are piled on her head. Whip cream and chocolate sauce are added for the finishing touches. Then a student with thick, long hair gets his head shaved.

There is more craziness. After those three acts are done, 30 students dressed in orange storm the court and promptly start doing a chicken dance, while polka music plays over the speakers. They flap their arms and shout, "Bawk, bawk, bawk," doing their best chicken imitation.

Suddenly, music turns to rock and the orange clothes are ripped off to reveal their true colors—green.

The crowd goes crazy.

Provo track coach Phil Olsen is also dressed up in orange shorts, a wig, and an orange T-shirt. Olsen discards the orange clothes to the green layer underneath. Then he runs around the court in an effort to get the crowd to do the wave.

There's more unusual entertainment. Next up is a chicken nugget eating contest between a representative from each class. There is a freshman, a sophomore, a junior, and a senior, and the goal is to see how many chicken nuggets they can cram into their mouth and still talk.

The occasion for all this craziness is Provo's upcoming game against Timpview that will be played later that night.

Drury is amused by all the attention and he gets into the spirit of the day. He wears a tie with an upside down dead chicken on it, compliments of his daughters.

Back to the entertainment. Next is a takeoff of the *Tonight Show's Jaywalking* with Jay Leno. A Provo student got loose at Timpview with a microphone and a camera. The following is his best attempt at imitating Jaywalking.

The first question is asked to a Timpview student.
When was the Revolutionary War?
Timpview student: 1912?
Another Timpview student: 1995?
Provo student: 1776.

Another pair of Timpview students are found and another question is asked.

What does G.P.A. stand for?
Timpview student: I don't know, but I think I have a .90.
Another Timpview student: I think it has something to do with NASA.
Provo student: Grade Point Average.

Final question: Who is the vice president of the United States?
Timpview student: Al Gore.
Another Timpview student: Al Rouker.
Provo student: Dick Cheney.

The assembly ends with a video that is played on a big screen.

There are highlights from the team's wins over Pleasant Grove, Mountain View, and Lone Peak. After the highlights of Tika Wesley scoring inside, Mick Hagen dribbling down the key, and Joey Pututau hitting a three-pointer, the video shows a row of dominoes, each with a name of a school Provo has beaten during the year. There is Mayfair, Lone Peak, Springville, Payson. In slow motion the dominoes bang into each other complete with the sound effects of rocks clanging into each other. The last domino is Timpview and in slow motion it falls.

A booming voice then asks the question, "Are you going to be there to see the next one fall?"

Fans pile out of the gym for the rest of their school day. There's a free barbecue lunch and a tailgate party scheduled for 5:30 p.m. with game time set for 7:00 p.m.

It's official. The countdown has begun. T-minus eight hours and counting, before the biggest game of the year, before the biggest game of their lives.

Provo comes into the game 14-0 and ranked No. 1. Thoughts of an undefeated season are on the team's mind.

"If I we were to go undefeated it would be so special, I couldn't even put it into words, but I realize the possibility of that happening is so small," Drury says. "Too many times I've seen teams go into the state tournament with glossy records, only to get beat. All I'm thinking about is we have a real good chance at being 15-0, that's all I'm thinking about."

Privately the players are very well aware that this game is the key to their undefeated chances. The T-Birds come into the game with a 13-1 record and are ranked No. 2 in the state. It's the first time the two schools have met at this point in the season when they have combined to have just one loss.

Even though Provo is undefeated and ranked No. 1, Drury believes Timpview is the favorite.

"We're the underdog, even though we are the only undefeated team left in the state (3A through 5A), everyone except in newspaper land knows we're the underdog," Drury said. "It's like when Arizona lost. All the sudden they're not No. 1, but everyone who knows college basketball, knows they were still No. 1."

The thought of Timpview being favored to beat Provo used to be laughable, but that could be said about any of Provo's opponents.

When Timpview opened its doors in 1977, it became the second high school in Provo.

Timpview would draw students from southwest Provo and north Provo, while Provo would get its students from east and west Provo.

Despite the geographic division, when the two schools split Provo kept the basketball talent, leaving Timpview's basketball program to start much like an expansion team with little experience and with minimal talent.

Timpview hired former Provo assistant Tim Lewis as its head coach. After posting two straight losing seasons, Lewis turned Timpview from an expansion program to a title contender. In Timpview's ninth year, Lewis coached the T-Birds to a region title. In his 11th and final season (1988) Lewis' expansion project was complete.

Matt Bowman, with help from Tim Lewis' son Quincy, completed a rare high school feat—an undefeated season. 25-0. Bowman averaged 28 points per game and scored 52 points in one game on 21 of 24 shooting from the field. Timpview was so dominating that only two of its 25 games were closer than 12 points.

Tim Lewis retired with a state championship and then watched his son Quincy lead Timpview to another one under new coach Don Chamberlain.

The T-Birds finished with a 22-3 record and won their second straight state championship. Two of Timpview's three losses that year were to Provo.

Since then, Timpview has rivaled Provo in basketball tradition. In 1999 Timpview beat Provo to win the 4A state championship. Don Chamberlain then retired and the Thunderbirds hired assistant Perry Wildeboer. In his first year Wildeboer guided Timpview to a 4A state championship.

Another argument for Timpview being the favorite is the fact that Timpview is on its longest winning streak over Provo in the history of the rivalry. The T-Birds have won six in a row.

For Provo the pressure to win is mounting.

Drury is told by some students, "This is my senior year. You have to beat Timpview. I can't lose to Timpview in my senior year."

Thanks for the vote of confidence.

Someone else tells him, "I don't care if you win another game all season, but you've got to beat Timpview."

Everyone he meets has something to say to him about the game. "You have to beat them. I have to go to church with those Timpview people."

Timpview offers a different challenge for Provo. Most teams that play Provo take the court questioning their confidence. History has proven they can't beat Provo—they never do.

If there's one team that is not intimidated by the rich Provo tradition, it's Timpview. Even though Provo has a commanding lead in the series (35-20), recent history has been a much different story. Provo won the first 15 games against Timpview when the rivalry began, but since then it's been a coin toss each time the two teams play.

Even with Timpview's six-game winning streak, Provo has won 20 games and Timpview has won 20 games after Provo dominated the early years of the rivalry.

Now the shoe is on the other foot. Provo finds itself in a precarious predicament. The Bulldogs wonder, can they beat Timpview? After all, the last time Provo beat Timpview, the seniors on this team were freshman.

But this is Provo's year. The student body can feel it. This is the team that will restore the proper order to the rivalry.

The student body is ready for the game, but the players still have some preparation to finish.

On Monday, the day before the Timpview game, coach Keli brings to practice what he calls the swat stick. It is a racquetball racket tapped to the end of a broom stick. On the white tape the words "Swat stick" are written in red.

Coach Keli holds it up in the air so it can easily reach over 10 feet. He got the idea after Provo played Mountain View and former Mountain View center Karl Riding blocked eight Provo shots. Today he calls it the Miles stick in honor of 6'10" Timpview center Chris Miles, who is a junior. Players have to get used to shooting over it.

As the team practices running its plays, Drury warns his post players, "I'm looking at which one of you (Tika or Tai) are going to have a sore jaw tomorrow. Tika, if you think Garrett (Groesbeck) fouls you, wait until (Ryan) Jackson elbows you. He's a nice kid and I'd like to have him as a neighbor, but on the court he's cheap."

Provo will run what it calls "anchor" for most of the night. That means Tai will stay home on defense in the low post, while the other players will matchup with their men.

After practice the team heads into the team room for a talk.

"I've heard people talking about THE GAME since last week. You can't get caught up in that. I'm not counting on being 25-0, I'm counting on being 15-0," Drury says. "I've had a couple of teams that got to this point undefeated and they got caught up in that and I think it hurt them.

"I honestly look at this game as just another game. I didn't want to beat anyone more than I did at Payson last week. Their coach has made it such a personal thing, like he won't be vindicated until he beats me. I'd just as soon beat Payson as Timpview, and I think we have a strong reason to beat American Fork and same with Orem, when they opened their new gym.

"Doesn't it seem like every time we take the floor, it's a special event or night for somebody? You guys have to rise above that. In my opinion they're (Timpview) the second best team in the state, next to us.

"I can't tell you who is going to win. You have to rebound, play defense and take good shots. Whoever does that the best will win, it's that simple."

Monday night the team gets together for its traditional team dinner. The team dinners are usually hosted by parents. All the Thursday nights have been spoken for, but on Monday nights before a game, the team is on its own. They usually meet at a restaurant. Tonight they meet at a Mexican restaurant called Cafe Rio.

While the players eat, the talk centers on guard Kade Koop, who has had some other things on his mind. Rumor has it a Pleasant Grove High School senior wants to fight Koop in a dispute over a girl. So Koop explains what happened on Saturday night.

He went out the front door and noticed a van was parked outside. Koop saw some shadowy figures moving around near the van. Koop thinks a rumble is about to go down, so he goes back in and calls for reinforcements. Soon, four carloads of friends show up and when they go out to approach the van, they are shocked to find the people in the van are Jehovah's Witnesses.

The team gets a good laugh out of Koop's story. Then their focus is turned to Timpview. It's clear the student bodies hate each other, but what about the players? How do the players feel about their rivals?

When asked to use one word to describe Timpview, the team takes turns.

Mercer: Asses.

Hagen: Courteous.

"Courteous," Pututau says. "Four of them are nice to you," Pututau says. "They were calling you needle dick."

In Hawaii, Hagen wore a white shirt under his uniform. The referee asked him to take it off. It turns out the shirt he was wearing under his uniform was a Timpview shirt.

Curtis Porter, the quarterback on the football team, has joined the players for dinner. He gives up his opinion: Swagger

Pututau: Chokers

Koop: Wannabes

Snarr: Cocky

Ady: Cocky

Stringham: neighbors (he lives in Timpview's boundaries).

T-Minus two hours and counting. It's 5 p.m. and Timpview coach Perry Wildeboer munches on a steak taco while he watches the JV game. He holds a clipboard that contains his pregame notes.

On the top of the list there are three names: Joey, Carter, and Hagen. Next to their names are two words: NO THREES.

Wildeboer's game plan is simple but complex. Take away Provo's outside shooting.

But how?

"I told our guys the Wesleys may have 24 and 16 points. That's fine. I'd rather have two of them play well than all five."

Wildeboer will overplay Provo's guards on the wing in an effort to take away the three-pointers.

"They're going to get some (threes). A loose ball bounces to someone and they'll take a shot, but we can't let them have good looks outside," Wildeboer explains.

The strategy is sound, mainly because Timpview has two players that will let the T-Birds get away with it. Senior Ryan Jackson is 6'5", and an excellent defender. At 6'10", Miles is an imposing presence inside. Timpview will let Jackson and Miles take the Wesleys one-on-one.

Now it's time to find out if Wildeboer's strategy will work.

The crowd arrives late. Just five minutes to tip-off and the Dawg Pound, which holds 2,800 fans, still has about 500 empty seats.

But the line outside is long, and by tip-off the place is packed and there is standing room only as people have crowded around the exits trying to watch the game.

Drury gives his team some last minute advice. "This team has progressed as much as any team I've dealt with. To be where you are is unbelievable," Drury says. "I'm ready to play. Are you guys ready?"

"Yeah!"

"Let's take a minute if you want to."

The players kneel down, and in quiet meditation and prayer pause for 30 seconds before they file out of the locker room and wait until the national anthem finishes. As they file through the doors of the gym, most of them slap the brick above the door where there is a phrase in green lettering: "Play like Champions Today."

The packed arena is unlike anything most of them have ever played in. The lights are dimmed and the spotlight comes on. The non-starting seniors are introduced.

Cor-bin Merrrr-cer, Steve Torkildson, Scotty Add-ie. He's used to having his name mispronounced, even by his own PA announcer.

The starters then take the stage. Joey Pututau, Mick Hagen, Tai Wesley, Tika Wesley, and Craig Stringham.

The game is underway. Hagen hits a jumper and Tika scores inside. Timpview starts the game cold from outside and doesn't score until Miles hits one of two free throws with 5:14 left in the quarter to make the score 4-1.

The Bulldogs then fall apart. They commit seven turnovers in the final five minutes of the quarter and finish with just six points.

Meanwhile, Timpview heats up with a three-pointer from Matt

Mortensen and a baskets from Brad Shumpert and Taylor Jackson.

At the end of the quarter, Timpview leads 8-6.

Fans from both sides continue to trade barbs with each other. What would a Timpview/Provo rivalry be if there weren't insults to trade?

When the two teams played in football, Provo fans yelled, "Steroids helped you," an insult aimed at Timpview's huge offensive line.

It didn't take long for Timpview fans to counter: "Steroids did nothing for you."

Tonight fans from each school take aim at each school's point guard. Timpview point guard Matt Pinegar, a junior, had been dating a girl named Mandy. Hagen took her out before the Timpview game.

For fans, this was too easy. When Pinegar touched the ball, Provo fans yelled, "Mandy's reject."

When Hagen dribbled, Timpview fans countered with, "Mandy's rebound."

Meanwhile, on the court Provo struggles to get any open shot. Pututau takes his only shot of the game, an airball. Tika scores once inside, but Miles swats his next shot away.

Pinegar takes over. He scores five points in the quarter and helps Timpview to a 15-12 half-time lead.

Both teams expected a defensive battle, but the low score surprised everyone.

In the locker room Drury is direct and to the point, but does not yell. He's come to the conclusion that this team won't respond if he screams.

"If we're going to score 24 (six points a quarter) and they're going to score 30, it looks to me like we're going to lose by six. You've got to do something about that."

With the offense stalled like a car in the middle of an intersection, the focus turns to Hagen. "Mick, you're lethargic. You look like you're out there studying for a math test. If you want to play like you're studying to retake the ACT test again, let us know because we can beat this team without you, but it will be easier for us to beat them with you. You've got to be more aggressive as an offensive player."

Drury then turns his attention to Timpview's point guard.

"If any of you are looking for a star, Pinegar is it. He is the best player on the floor. He is breaking us down. We have to stop Pinegar's penetration and get back when he kicks it out."

Schoonover points out one of the positives of the first half.

"We played terrible in the first half and we're still right in it. We really can't play any worse."

The third quarter is underway and Timpview has a greeting for Provo—a Pinegar three-pointer. Timpview continues on a 9-0 run to take control of the game. After Taylor Jackson comes up with a steal and a layup, Timpview leads 24-12 with 4:10 left in the the quarter and Provo still hasn't scored.

By the end of the third quarter, there's only smoke lingering from the bomb Timpview dropped. The T-Birds lead is 30-17. They have come into Provo's house, sat down, and kicked their feet up on the furniture.

Embarrassed by its performance, Provo finally makes a run. The final quarter opens with a basket from Tika, but Timpview gets a free throw from Pinegar, followed by a jumper from Pinegar that gives the T-Birds a 33-19 lead.

Enter junior Tai Wesley. He's about to show Division I schools why they are justified in recruiting him. He converts a three-point play and after Pinegar answers for Timpview, he counters with two free throws, followed by a bucket inside the paint.

But Timpview has many weapons. Sophomore Matt Mortensen hits a three-pointer that looks like it puts the game out of reach, but Hagen won't let Provo's comeback die. He scores five straight points, and Tai adds another basket to cut the lead to 38-33 with 2:50 left in the game.

Taylor Jackson then makes one of two free throws for Timpview, but the Bulldogs get a huge shot from Carter, who drains a three-pointer from the corner.

Suddenly, Timpview's 14-point fourth-quarter lead is down to three at 39-36 with 1:31 left in the game.

After the two teams trade free throws, Provo has a chance to tie the game, but Hagen's three-pointer goes in and out. No problem, Tai is there to recycle the miss and cut the lead to 42-41 with 12 seconds left in the game.

Provo then calls a timeout before Timpview can inbound the ball. The game is going down to the final seconds, just the way it is scripted. Another classic.

Drury sets up a full-court, man-to-man press. The Bulldogs don't want Pinegar to get his hands on the ball. In an effort to cover Pinegar, guard Andrew Low is alone under the basket. He gets the ball and races upcourt. Provo can't catch him. Tika, the player who is left to defend the basket, comes up to defend him, but he dishes off to Ryan Shumpert, who scores a layup.

Wait! There's still time. Provo rushed the ball inbounds and in desperation gets the ball to Tai, who has had the hot hand all game. Three, two, one, Tai is on the right wing, a step behind the three-point line. He lets it fly.

Buzzzzzzz, the horn sounds.

Clank.

The ball hits the rim and bounces away. Timpview fans celebrate in wild fashion. A sea of orange swarms the court as Timpview fans take advantage of the opportunity to rub it in.

The T-Birds have done it again and of all places they have done it in the Dawg Pound.

The gloating, the finger waving, the taunting. If there's one thing that high school students have never learned is sportsmanship. Police quickly get in position to separate the two student bodies. The frustration of Provo losing to Timpview again, coupled with Timpview fans celebrating on Provo's court has Bulldog fans in a fighting mood.

The one bright spot for Provo was the play of Tai, who scored 12 of his 17 points in the fourth quarter. Tika finished with 11 points as Wildeboer's game plan worked to perfection.

He was willing to give up some points inside the paint if it meant shutting down Provo's guards.

Pututau was held scoreless and took just one shot. Hagen never got it going. He had nine points. For some reason, Hagen admits, he doesn't have the energy he normally does and he doesn't know why.

On the other hand, Pinegar killed Provo. His penetration through Provo's defense and his shooting was the difference. He finished with 16 points.

In a quiet locker room, Drury takes off his Timpview chicken tie. His dress shirt is untucked as he writes on the board.

1) They made us spectate on our "O"

2) We were passive. No urgency.

As Drury writes on the board, the cheers coming from Timpview's locker room can be heard through the walls.

"The best team won tonight. Had we won I wouldn't have been pleased. You shouldn't have won," Drury says. "I'm disappointed in the way you attacked. I'm not disappointed in the loss. You were building to a loss, it was inevitable."

Now it's coach Keli's turn. "No heart, you guys have no heart. You guys let them come in here an embarrass you on your own floor. You've got to take care of business here."

Drury ends the post game talk by writing one more word on the board.

URGENCY.

Over the last 14 games, Drury has felt it slowly slipping out of the team's grip. Now it cost the team in the biggest game of the year.

The loss left Provo to do some soul searching. So this is how it feels to lose. Why of all teams did it have to be Timpview? Maybe we're not the best team in the state. How good are we?

So many questions.

On a January night, one Provo dream disappeared in a wave of orange. There will be no undefeated season for Provo, and they will be waving goodbye to the No. 1 ranking. The one game that mattered the most, the one they wanted to win at all costs, had eluded them.

They say athletics mirrors life. The lessons that can be learned playing sports are ones that can be applied to life.

Lesson number one. How do you rebound from devastating setback? Next up on the schedule is a talented American Fork team that figured to contend for the Region 6 title. Would this loss be the beginning of the end? Has Provo peaked?

For the first time all year, Provo's resolve would be tested and the Bulldogs would have to play their next opponent after having their confidence shaken.

CHAPTER ELEVEN

A WESLEY FAMILY BASKETBALL TRADITION

The Timpview loss weighed on Tika Wesley's mind. He tried to get to bed at 11 p.m., but nothing doing.

At midnight his eyes were still wide open. At 1 a.m he hadn't even let out a yawn and by 2 a.m. he quit trying to sleep and got up.

He grabbed the keys to the car and drove to IHOP where he nodded when the waitress asked, "Table for one?"

Wesley sat and tried to eat away his misery. More pancakes please. As far as losses go, this one stuck to him like syrup to the handle of a fork. He skipped a family get-together with his parents' friends, who were visiting from Guam. He wasn't in the mood to socialize.

When Provo loses, no one takes it harder than Tika Wesley. He's the team's low-post presence, the person the offense revolves around. He is the heartbeat of Provo. His smile is unmistakable when the team wins and his scowl is inescapable when the team loses.

He is a 6'5" 230-pound senior, a few inches short of a "can't miss Division I prospect," but any absence of height is more than made up for in heart.

The one constant in Provo High basketball has always been a big man. Someone to feed the ball to when the outside shots aren't falling. Someone who can score in the clutch. Someone who Drury can run a play to and get a good shot or at least some free throws.

This year Tika Wesley is Provo's go-to big man. He is the fourth Wesley to go through Provo's program.

Susan and Hiagi Wesley already had three boys—Mekeli, Russell and T.G. when they got the news that another Wesley was on the way. It was Tika.

The Wesleys took a trip from their home in Figi to American Samoa to visit some relatives. Tika surprised his parents by coming ahead of schedule. He arrived in December in Samoa during the trip instead of January in Figi when he was supposed to.

The family left Figi for West Jordan, Utah when Tika was two. Nearly two years later the family moved again from West Jordan to Orem.

But the family's stay in Orem didn't last long. Three years later, when Tika was seven, the Wesleys moved to Guam, where Tika still has many fond memories.

The family looked for a house they could afford and settled on a three bedroom house with a tin roof and wooden floors right behind a bar called Susie's Tavern—no relation to Tika's mother, Susan.

"That place was a dump, man. If you would have seen it, you would be astounded how run down it was," Mekeli said. "But there was a hill behind us and the beach was only a few hundred yards away."

The house was on one side of the road and the ocean was on the other, but it wasn't exactly paradise. Perhaps the reason why the Wesleys got a good deal was the locals thought the house was haunted.

"People would always tell us stories about the white lady ghost that would appear on the hill. We looked for her, but we never saw her. We did see some wild stuff," Mekeli added. "One time a typhoon came in and dad thought our house wouldn't make it, so we went to stay with some neighbors. When we got back, a big mango tree in our front yard had been uprooted, but the house was still there."

The Wesleys may not have seen any ghosts, but they did have some unwanted guests. Sometimes hermit crabs would crawl into the house and snakes would sometimes get tangled up in the power lines and knock out the power.

"I'd look down and there would be tons of termites eating away at the wood floor," Tika said.

When you're from a family of nine (six boys, one girl), there are never enough bathrooms, especially when it's monsoon season and water is scarce. So the Wesley boys figured out if they plugged the rain gutter over the garage with a tennis ball, they had a built-in water softener.

One of the boys, usually the youngest brother Keli'i, would get up on the roof to take out the tennis ball and bingo, they had a shower. When they were done, Keli'i would be sent back on the roof and put the tennis ball back in the rain gutter for next time.

The Wesley family soon found a nicer residence and moved out of their house behind Susie's Tavern, but the family was still in for another change. Older brother Mekeli was struggling in school and was having trouble fitting in.

"He was taller than most of the other kids, so they decided they wanted to fight him," Tika says.

Mekeli was also excelling in basketball and Guam wasn't the place to play for a serious player, so the Wesleys explored their options. A family friend, Keli Lobendahn, was living in Orem and coaching at Provo High School.

Hmm. This had potential.

Arrangements were made and soon Wesley was sent to live with the Lobendahns, just weeks after he had already started his 9th grade year in Guam.

"In Figi they start you early in school, so I was ahead when I came to Orem. We had a meeting with Drury and coach Keli to decide what grade to put me in," Mekeli said. "They decided it would be best to put me in with my age group. I don't think I would have had nearly the career I had if I had come as a junior."

Even though the Lobendahn family lived in Mountain View boundaries, Mekeli never thought twice about what high school to attend. He was living with the Lobendahns so he would go to Provo where coach Keli could oversee his transition.

"It was pretty crowded. They have nine kids, one had already married and was out of the house, but there was 10 of them plus me," Mekeli said. "I shared a room with Ono (Kerisiano), who also played on the high school team."

Even though the Lobendahn house was already crowded, there was always room for one more.

"I bought some 2x4's and made a bunk bed and he shared a room with Kerisiano," coach Keli said. "When he got here he was very raw, about as raw as anyone we get in our system, but he was 6'4". He was a good learner and was willing to put in hours."

In Mekeli's sophomore year, his stock was on the rise like the tide in front of a Guam typhoon. His family had moved to Orem, just in time to see him help Provo win a state 4A title in 1995.

Mekeli finished off his Provo career in impressive style. As a senior he averaged 19.6 points and 11 rebounds per game and helped Provo to another state title.

In the championship game he scored 21 points on 8 of 11 shooting. He also grabbed nine rebounds and blocked four shots in Provo's 45-29 win over East High School.

Mekeli now had one championship ring for his left hand and one for his right. Two state championships in three years.

The Wesley/Provo tradition had begun, and Mekeli had caught the attention of college coaches. At 6'9", he had a soft touch outside and felt equally comfortable posting up—a rare combination.

Even though Wesley played in Utah, talk of his game spread around the country. In one day Mekeli got 69 letters from colleges. He had so much mail, it took two apple boxes to store all of his letters. The schools most interested in him were mostly in the West—schools like Washington, Washington State, USC, Oregon, Pepperdine, Weber State, San Diego St., BYU, Loyola-Marymount, and Hawaii, but Marquette, Old Dominion, and LSU also threw their hats into the ring.

Gradually, he narrowed his choices to Hawaii, Colorado State, and BYU. He was learning toward Colorado State where coach Stew Morrill was the head coach at the time. Morrill and Drury were teammates at Provo High in 1970.

But the family wanted Mekeli to choose BYU and stay close to home so they could watch him play. They had already missed out on most of his sophomore year when they were still in Guam and didn't want to miss any more highlights.

So on a Sunday night in early April of 1996 he signed early with BYU near the end of his junior year.

"I remember some of my teammates were upset with me," Mekeli said. "If I wouldn't have signed early, there would have been recruiters in the stands and that would have given guys like

Gabe Rhoades and Jeremy Frampton more exposure. But I didn't want to worry about getting injured or having a bad season, so I took the offer."

Wesley started for BYU as a freshman, but the program had bottomed out. BYU got off to a 1-6 record and fired coach Roger Reid. The team went on to post its worst mark in school history with a 1-25 record.

Steve Cleveland was hired and the rebuilding process began. By the time Mekeli was a senior, he led BYU to a Mountain West Tournament title and an NCAA tournament berth.

But BYU's success in the Mountain West Conference and a trip to the NCAA tournament didn't do much for Wesley's pro prospects.

"Looking back on it, I feel really blessed having the career I did at BYU, but people tell me if I had gone to Utah and had the career I did, I would have been a first round pick. There are other schools that will promote you better, obviously the bigger the conference the more looks you get. I wish I could have had a better shot, but I am undersized and in-between positions."

Mekeli spent the 2003 season playing in Belgium and is hopeful someday he can play in the NBA, but until then he's happy where he is.

"Belgium is awesome. Everyone speaks English," Mekeli said. "The first year I played overseas, I was in Spain where the only people in the country who knew English were the missionaries and some road trips were 15 hour bus rides. In Belgium there's only two teams that are more than two hours away."

Belgium is proving to be easier on his family life that has now grown. His daughter Mia turned five in 2003 and his son Keliano—the name is a cross and a tribute to coach Keli and Ono turned two.

Mekeli believes he has the ability to play in the NBA, but is also realistic enough to know it may never happen.

"I see players I've played against and done fairly well against who are playing in the NBA, and that makes me hope for another shot," Mekeli added. "Still, there are things in my game I need to work on, but yeah I do think I can compete and play. I want to play as long as somebody allows me to. With the team I'm with in Belgium, I could probably play for another 15 years. It's a good situ-

Tika Wesley gets ready to make a move against Pleasant Grove's Trent Jeppsen and Nathan Clement (No. 44), while Samantha Olsen (left) and Shantae Briggs look on in the background.

ation out there, almost to the point where it was boring. I was there eight and a half months. I got there in the end of August and left April 28. We played 26 official games. If you get in the right situation you can make big bucks. I've seen contracts with guys who play in Greece, Turkey, and Spain that pay $1.5 million net. The highest paid guy in Belgium makes $350,000."

Mekeli's two younger brothers, Russell and T.G., would follow in his footsteps, but neither one would have the impact Mekeli did. Russell, 6'4", a late bloomer, was a junior when Provo won its second straight title in 1998. He came off the bench as a senior.

After Russell graduated from Provo, he walked on at Utah Valley State College and made the team. He redshirted in 2003 and was in UVSC's plans to make the jump from a junior college program to a Division I program beginning in the 2003-04 season.

T.G. didn't play college basketball. He's 6'5" and two years younger than Russell. During T.G.'s senior year, Tika was the one who would sub in for T.G. when he was in foul trouble or needed a rest.

Tai is a junior and is 6'7", and has the best chance to catch Mekeli in height and is a better Division I prospect than Tika.

The reason? Primarily because Tai is two inches taller than Tika, which falls into the old coaches slogan, "You can't teach height."

What difference does two inches make?

Plenty. Height discrimination is alive and well in college basketball.

That's one reason players are routinely listed a few inches taller than they really are on rosters, programs, or media guides.

A 6'7" post player can find a spot on many teams, while 6'5" post players can be found everywhere. There's not a lot of Division I schools that are looking for 6'5" post players.

Still, there is plenty of interest in Tika.

After one game, Matt Logan, Salt Lake Community College assistant coach, talked to Drury about Tika's game.

Logan: Have you ever seen a better player pass out of the post?

Drury: Yes.

Logan: Did you see Bill Walton play or something?

Drury: No, his brother Mekeli was pretty good.

Logan: I watched Mekeli play. I think Tika is better (at passing out of the post). I brought down the head coach Norm Parrish and he was impressed.

Salt Lake Community College would take him right now, but Wesley isn't committing to anything yet. He's going to wait to see what his options are when the season is over.

Tika is not shy but is often reserved. He's not a loudmouth and has a sensitive side. On his mother's birthday, he bought flowers for her and before practice drove to the travel agency where she works to surprise her.

He's also a favorite with the coaches. They love his hard work. They love his competitiveness. They love his no excuse attitude. Give a coach 12 Tika Wesleys and he would show you a state championship.

If he has a weakness it would be free-throw shooting and his outside shooting, but the team doesn't need him to shoot outside.

Portland State assistant coach Barrett Perry was at one of Provo's home games. When asked who he was looking at, Perry said, "Tika. Who else is good?"

Portland State wouldn't be the only team looking at Tika, if he were only a few inches taller.

With his shoes off, Tika Wesley is 6'5".

Tai has gotten letters from Oregon, BYU, UC Irvine, and several other schools, but just how much interest there is in him is hard to tell. Most schools send out hundreds of letters a year to prospective recruits even though they may only have a few scholarships.

Tika scores more points, averages more rebounds, and shoots a better field-goal percentage, so why are more schools interested in his little brother Tai?

Two reasons. Tai's a junior, which means he has an upside, and he's taller and has a wider wingspan.

Even though they're similar, they are different. Tika doesn't like to displease his coach.

"Approval is important to him. He's more serious, more organized, and less outgoing than Tai," Susan Wesley said. "Tika never wanted to do anything that would get the coach to yell at him, while Tai didn't care if the coach yelled at him. It was like 'oh well.'"

Tai Wesley powers inside for a basket past Pleasant Grove's Scott Valgardson (No. 33 and Todd Thurgood (No. 3).

Tika is clean. Tai's a slob.

Tika is Tony Randall, Tai is Jack Klugman.

"Tika is like a girl. He cleans his room. All of his clothes are folded and the labels are showing," Tai said.

They have their differences at home, but on the court they are quite similar. Like Tika, it wasn't too long ago when Tai's game consisted of mostly rebounding. In seventh and eighth grade he averaged about four points a game and those were mostly on offensive rebound baskets. But as a freshman, Tai saw how good Mekeli had become and wanted to emulate his older brother.

Tai once said he didn't want to go to BYU because Mekeli went to BYU and didn't get any serious professional looks. He wants to go to a big-time school where he can be taken seriously as an NBA prospect.

Tai not only wants to keep up with his brothers, he wants to surpass them.

When he was just two, he would ride his bike around with his brothers, but the stupid training wheels were slowing him down, so he asked his mother to take them off so he could go faster and keep up with his brothers.

Mom, sensing it was too dangerous said no.

Not satisfied with the answer, Tai went to Mekeli and got his way. Mekeli took off the training wheels and Tai was soon cruising up and down the street.

Tai was now free to catch up to his brothers, and he's been chasing them ever since.

CHAPTER TWELVE

PROVO TRADITION—WE BLEED GREEN

Provo's Emily Durrant banks in a 10-footer off the glass. About 15 rows up from the scorers table, Emily's father Devin Durrant smiles his approval. Devin Durrant rarely cheers, he never yells, but often smiles.

Durrant can often be seen watching Provo High School games. He'll stroll past the scorers table and up the stairs to a seat about half way up the bleachers until he finds a good seat in the middle, like he's at the movies.

This isn't the place where he played. Since Durrant graduated from Provo High School in 1978, the school has built a new wing that includes a 2,500 seat gym. The old historic gym is now host to junior varsity and sophomore games.

If there was ever a doubt that Devin's playing days were long ago, there's a constant reminder. The seasons of his life have changed some of his brown hair to a light shade of gray like the leaves changing color in the fall.

Another reminder is his daughter Emily. She used to be so cute running around in her diaper when Durrant was with the Indiana Pacers.

Now when she walks by, she turns heads. She's 5'10" (125 pounds, just a guess) and looks better in street clothes than she does in her basketball uniform.

Emily played for Provo High School just like her dad. She graduated in 2001. Her success at Provo High makes it so easy to reminisce about her father. Her bank shot off the glass is like a flashback to 1978.

When sports writers say Allen Iverson was in the Zone because he scored 34 points, it pales in comparison to what Durrant did on March 5, 1978.

Durrant scored the first 11 points of the game against American Fork. He made 15 of his first 17 shots he took and by the time he'd led Provo to a 52-45 win, he'd tallied 38 points to go along with 12 rebounds. He only missed five shots all night.

It was Wilt Chamberlin-esk.

Durrant would do it again and again. In another game against American Fork, a 66-61 win, he scored 41 points on 17 of 23 shooting from the field and pulled down 10 rebounds.

Nights like those were not unusual for Durrant. In a 74-35 win against Payson, Durrant outscored the Lions by himself. He had 37 points.

"In one game against Cedar City he was 16 for 16 in his field goals," said Durrant's coach Jim Spencer. "When we played Highland, they ran a full-court press. We just gave it to Devin and everyone cleared out."

Durrant, a 6'7" forward, finished his senior season by averaging 31.5 points, 14 rebounds, six assists, and four blocks per game while helped Provo to a 26-0 record and a state championship.

"My sophomore and junior years we lost in the semis, so to win it all in my senior year was a lot of fun," Durrant said. "I had great teammates who were unselfish and coach (Jim) Spencer allowed me to shine. It's very difficult to get four other guys to go along with a system like that (featuring Durrant), but they were great."

Durrant was invited to the Kentucky/Indiana vs. U.S. All-Stars game where he scored 18 points and grabbed eight rebounds in the all-star game and stunned many by winning the one-on-one contest.

Durrant continued his career at BYU, which is literally across the street from Provo High. Durrant finished third in all-time scoring at BYU.

He averaged 27.9 points per game as a senior at BYU. Perhaps most impressive was the fact that he never shot less than 50 percent from the field in any of his four years at BYU.

If the mark of a great player is he makes others around him better, then Durrant fits the definition. In his four-year college career,

BYU won three WAC championships and made three NCAA tournament appearances.

In 1983 he helped team USA to a bronze medal in the World Games. He led Team USA with 23 points in the tournament opener against Peru. Pretty impressive considering Durrant's teammates included Karl Malone, Charles Barkley, and his roommate for the tournament, Kevin Willis, who won a ring with the San Antonio Spurs in 2003.

In the process, Durrant caught the attention of the NBA.

Los Angeles Lakers General Manager Jerry West said, "You have to like a lot of things about him. He can really score. He's a fine passer. He's very composed. He's a great kid."

NBA Scouting Director Marty Blake called Durrant the best small forward in the country.

"He's probably the best (small forward) I've seen in 10 years at moving without the ball. He'll be a small forward in the NBA. A (John) Drew, a (Adrian) Dantley, a (Mark) Aguirre or a (Bernard) King."

Durrant was picked by the Indiana Pacers in the second round of the 1984 NBA draft, but he never got to display his shooting touch. He averaged 5.1 points per game in his only season with Indiana.

"I was a little star-struck. One night I'm playing against Larry Bird and the next I'm playing against Dominique Wilkins, then Julius Irving, who was my boyhood idol," Durrant said. "Indiana was losing and they didn't have time to wait around for a rookie,. They had to make some moves."

Durrant was released after one season, but signed with the Phoenix Suns where he says he played his best basketball.

"I loved playing in Phoenix. I scored 27 points in a preseason game, but Jerry Colangelo (Suns owner) wanted to bring in a player from Europe, Georgi Glouchkov, who was the first European player at the time. They had plenty of small forwards, so they cut me four games into the season."

Durrant played two seasons in Europe before calling it a career. He now lives in Provo and is involved with property management.

Inside his Provo home there are several scrapbooks and folders filled with photos and faded newspaper articles that his wife Julie has organized.

There's a picture of him accepting the No. 1 Award sponsored by Hertz. The person giving him the trophy is O.J. Simpson. There's a copy of *Sports Illustrated* with a toothless Leon Spinks smiling about his win over Muhammed Ali. Durrant made the section "Faces in the crowd."

When you mention Provo High School basketball history, Durrant is one of the first names that will roll off someone's tongue.

His brother Mark also played at BYU and now does color commentary for BYU games on KSL radio.

Seeing Durrant watching from the stands, along with other famous Provo alumni like Vance Law and Mekeli Wesley, begs the question: Just who is the greatest player in Provo history?

Let the debate begin.

If this was a poll question on the high school web site, the frontrunners would be Durrant or Brett Vroman.

Vroman, a 6'11" center, was the key to Provo's incredible string of 54 straight wins. In Vroman's junior and senior years, Provo never lost a game.

"He was the No. 2 player in the country (1974) and the No. 1 player was Moses Malone," Drury said. "John Wooden came to his front door."

Vroman had letters from over 200 schools. He averaged 20 points, 15 rebounds, and eight blocked shots per game during his senior year. He narrowed his choices to Maryland, BYU, Utah, and UCLA.

In the end John Wooden won out and Vroman played at UCLA in 1974-75, which was the last national championship team for Wooden. The following season, Vroman' s sophomore season, UCLA finished third in the country with a 27-5 record, but Vroman wasn't happy and who could blame him?

He played in just 22 games and averaged 1.9 points per game. He took just 31 shots—for the entire season. So he transferred to UNLV to play for Jerry Tarkanian. After two years at UNLV, Vroman was drafted in the fourth round of the 1978 draft by the Philadelphia 76ers. He never played for Philadelphia. Instead he found a career overseas. He did play briefly in the NBA in 1980-81, but that included just 11 games with the Jazz.

Vroman may have been the center of attention during Provo's record-breaking run, but he wasn't a one-man team. He was in pretty good company. Gifford Nielsen, who was a key to Provo's undefeated season in 1973, led the team in scoring with 19.6 points per game. He then made a name for himself at quarterback when he led the nation in passing yards and touchdowns in his junior year at BYU. Nielsen played for the Houston Oilers and is now a sportscaster for a Houston TV station.

"I don't have a problem talking about it (greatest player in Provo history), I just don't include myself," Durrant said. "Brett Vroman and Gifford Nielsen were both great players, and Vance Law was one of the best, he was an excellent basketball player. Then more recently Mekeli Wesley and one of my favorites, my brother Mark. He was a great Bulldog."

Law played a crucial role in Provo's undefeated season in 1974. He ultimately chose baseball like his father Vernon, who was a Cy Young Award winner with the Pittsburgh Pirates. Vance was an all-star for the Chicago Cubs in 1988 when he hit .289 with 11 home runs and 78 RBI for the Cubs. He would end up playing for five different teams over his 11-year Major League career.

The list of great players who have worn a Provo uniform goes on like the championship banners in the gym. There was Don Overly, who went on to play at BYU in 1940. Dave Lewis, Paul Kitchen, and Russ Jones all played for BYU in 1956. Lynn Gleave helped Provo to a state championship in 1956. Jim Reece (1966) was a three-year starter and ended up playing football at Utah.

Then there was Stew Morrill, who is now the head coach at Utah State. Morrill was a two-time All-Big Sky player while at Gonzaga. He then played professionally in Europe before beginning his coaching career. In Morrill's first four years at Utah State he won 94 games, the most wins a Utah State coach had ever had in history in their first four years. He was named "Big West Coach of the Year" in 2002.

Drury was also a big-time player. He started as a sophomore and led the team in scoring and rebounding. After his high school career was over, he joined BYU's program.

Steve Pinegar averaged 26 points per game in his junior year and 22 points per game as a senior before signing with Utah State. When approached on the subject Pinegar said his teammate Kelly Gardner deserves consideration.

More recently there was David Heaton, whom Drury called the best player on the 1981 championship team, and Brian Santiago.

Santiago was inducted into the Utah Valley State College Hall of Fame after he become just one of four players in school history to led the team in scoring (17.7) and assists (7.6) for a season. After his two years at UVSC, Santiago transferred to Fresno State where he set the single season assist record with 223 and was an All-WAC selection.

Then there were Kevin Nielsen and Greg Ballif, who both played at BYU. Veryl Law (1974-77), Vance's older brother, and Drury says as far as senior seasons go, Kris Cox (1995) was up there with the best and any list that didn't include David Liddiard (1993) wouldn't be complete.

"He (Liddiard) dominated at a position that was the hardest position to dominate in," Drury said. "It's easier to dominate at the point guard or center position, but he dominated at the wing position, the hardest position to dominate a game."

Overall, 34 Provo players have taken their game to BYU after graduating from Provo High School, which is by far the most from any other high school.

Regardless of who you pick, what player you label the "best ever," you can't be wrong even if you pick B.J. Chandler (1993) because there's no right or wrong answer.

"You can't compare generations because the game has changed. Alan Frampton is the best player I ever coached. He led the team in scoring for three straight years and as a senior he led the team in rebounding at point guard," Drury said. "I didn't coach Durrant, but I would think you would say you'd have to say Durrant would be up there."

Frampton played at BYU (1990), then later transferred to BYU-Hawaii. He helped Provo to an undefeated season in 1985.

Drury didn't coach Durrant, but he did coach Mekeli Wesley, who helped Provo to a pair of state championships in 1995 and 1997.

Wesley played at BYU and as a senior was the Mountain West Conference "Player of the Year. "

"If I had to list a top five, I would base the criteria on three things. He would have to have a good high school career, a good senior season, and a good college career," Drury said.

"Based on that criteria, I would say Alan Frampton, Mekeli Wesley, Brain Santiago, Eric Jackson, and David Liddiard."

As difficult as it is to name the best player, it's also just as tough to settle on which team was the best.

The most obvious are the ones who never lost a game. How can you do better than that?

The candidates are: The 1973, 1974, 1978, and 1985 Bulldogs. Wait, we must also consider the 1987, 1997, and 1998 teams.

The 1973, 1974, and 1985 teams all went undefeated. The 1987 team went 23-1 and won a state championship. Both the 1997 and 1998 teams went 23-2 and both won state championships.

The favorite would have to be the 1973 or 1974 team. In 1973 Provo went 25-0 and won the state title with the lineup of Vance and Veryl Law, Gifford Nielsen, Dave Card, Kory Sorensen, and Brett Vroman.

It was a team that would feature three professional athletes on it. Vance Law (baseball), Nielsen (football), and Vroman (basketball). Two other players went on to play at four-year colleges: Veryl Law and Sorensen.

"I'm probably a little biased, but we had a 6'-11" center and four other guys who played college ball. I don't know of too many teams who have that kind of depth," Vance Law said.

In 1974, Provo repeated as state champs and extended its winning streak to 49 straight games. Vroman played in the state tournament with a stress fracture in his foot. He was joined by Kelly Gardner, Mark Bowen, Kevin Ludlow and Dave Stewart. Steve Pinegar, a sophomore, was coming off the bench.

"The best team ever no doubt was in my sophomore year (1974). It's probably the best team ever in high school basketball," Pinegar said. "We had such a good balance. There was Durrant's years and the Santiago boys, forget that. I don't know what coach Spencer would say, but he'd be crazy to disagree."

Provo's 1985 team also went undefeated and won a state title. Led by Frampton, who was the state MVP, and Kevin Santiago.

But before the ballots are cast, there are two other teams to consider. Drury says the best team he had might have been the 1997 team, which went 23-2 and was ranked as high as 12th in the nation. The team beat Miami Senior, who was ranked second in the country at the time. Provo's two losses were no slouches. The Bulldogs lost to the nation's No. 1 ranked team and to Timpview.

"That team (1997) played three of the top 10 teams in the country and beat two of them," Drury said. "That team put the 1998 team on the platform."

Provo had another dominating run, winning three state championships in four years. By today's standard's with today's competition, it was amazing.

The Bulldogs won the title in 1995 and again in 1997. Mekeli Wesley started at center on both the 1995 and 1997 teams.

"I sat in between Vance and Veryl Law when we watched Provo with Mekeli (Wesley) and they asked me, 'Coach, do you think this team could beat our team?' I said, 'Nah.' We all agreed."

Provo won the state championship again the year after Wesley graduated (1998)—the third title in four years. Even though Wesley was gone, the team was loaded. Four players went onto play college basketball, including the oldest Wesley, Mekeli (BYU), Jake Chrisman (BYU), Jeremy Frampton (BYU-Hawaii), and Eric Jackson (Cal-Poly San Luis Obisbo).

While people debate over who had the best team and who was the best player, the one constant, overriding factor that helped turn out so many championships teams has been coaching.

Provo has had just five coaches in its history. Dolan Condie coached for 17 years from 1952-69. He won a state championship in 1956. He finished with a 248-92 overall record and a 148-39 league mark.

At one time under Condie, Provo won 47 straight league games.

How do you follow that record?

With a coach by the name of Jim Spencer, who compiled 478 career wins.

Under Spencer, Provo became the dominant program in the state. Spencer coached Provo to five state championships (second most in state history).

Steve Hodson, the former Orem High School guard went on to win three state championships as a high school coach, two at Cedar City (1994, 1995) and one at Canyon View (1999). He also worked as an assistant coach at Southern Utah.

Hodson took over the girls program at Canyon View that had lost 25 straight region games. His first year he turned the program around and helped Canyon View to an 11-10 overall record and a state tournament appearance for the first time in school history.

He's become an accomplished coach and is still an admirer of what Provo has been able to do.

"Just go check the records of how many high schools have never won a state championship. Each of them (Spencer and Drury) have won five. He (Drury) along with coach Spencer have put together an amazing defense. Over the years, I think a lot of teams have had trouble scoring on defense. That's been their biggest strength."

Spencer's legend began when he coached the Bulldogs to a phenomenal record. Over a three year period (1972-1975), Provo won 54 games and was just three wins shy of matching a national record before Granite beat Provo on December 3, 1975.

"It was a real relief when it ended," Spencer said. "Every game the boys didn't want to be the team to suffer the first loss. They didn't deserve that."

Granite scored the first 10 points of the game and held on for a stunning 47-42 upset.

"It was the worst game of our lives. I only had eight points, the lowest I've ever scored," said Provo guard Steve Pinegar, who was a junior when Granite snapped Provo's winning streak. "They just shocked us. We thought we would roll over them."

After the loss, Provo quickly started a new winning streak, reeling off 20 straight wins. One of those was a rematch with Granite in the first round of the state tournament.

This time the Bulldogs were ready. Sophomore Kim Garrett led the team with 22 rebounds.

Provo didn't have long to celebrate because Highland upset

Provo 68-66 in the next game, ending the Bulldogs season with a quarterfinal loss.

Still, Provo's record of 54 in a row is a mark that coaches today wonder if it will ever be broken.

"It's very rare to go undefeated in region, so I think it will be very difficult for any team to break their (Provo) streak," said former Mountain View coach Rob Cuff. "The most we ever won was 17 in a row. The better teams now will go out of state to play some of the top teams in the country. The only way I could see it happening is if a 1A or 2A school has a dynasty and doesn't play some of the bigger schools."

The winning streak is yet another monument to Spencer, who retired in 1982, but his legacy is still making an impact today.

"I felt like coach Spencer taught me a lot about basketball and about hard work. He deserves a lot of credit for any success I've had," said Vance Law, who is now BYU's baseball coach. "He told me that if I would shoot 10,000 shots over the next few months I would play a lot, so I went out and did it."

Durrant echoed Law's comments.

"He was a marvelous coach. One of his greatest skills was to get us to believe in ourselves. He instilled in us the confidence that we expected to win," Durrant said. "When I moved back from Kentucky, he called us all together and told us that we were the UCLA of high school basketball. Our warmups were just like UCLA's, except the colors."

Spencer was a big fan of UCLA legendary coach John Wooden and would often implement some of Wooden's philosophies in Provo.

"Jim was a Wooden fan from day one. He made us all read his (Wooden's) book," said Don Chamberlain, who was an assistant coach under Spencer before replacing Tim Lewis (another Provo assistant) as head coach at Timpview. "Wooden at the time was using a 2-2-1 press that was pretty effective, so we used it. He (Spencer) worked hard at it (coaching). He put in the extra time. He had great athletes, but he made some that way too."

Spencer can still be seen once in a while at Provo High School games. He slips in quietly and sits near the top in the bleachers and watches what he helped create.

"I will always have green flowing through me the rest of my life," Spencer added. "Craig's (Drury) successes are successes to me and his sorrow is sorrow to me."

Now that Spencer looks back on his coaching days, if he was giving a clinic, the subject would be clear: Be positive.

"When I started winning games, it was when I put my arms around the players and gave them positive reinforcement," Spencer said. "I told them they were the best and I let them know I trusted them."

Even now, nearly two decades after he retired, Spencer can still motivate people. His message is more relevant now than it was in the 1970s.

"There was a British commander who was once asked what he would change if he could change anything and he said, 'I would give more praise.' As I look back on my life I would be like that British commander," Spencer said. "I would give more praise. I guarantee you, it would pay off."

CHAPTER THIRTEEN

GREEN WITH ENVY

On paper, Payson High School is a state title contender every year.

In the summer Payson looks like it could go ahead and order the state championship rings.

But there is one constant about Payson basketball. When the season starts, the Lions always lose to Provo.

When asked what his record is against Payson, Drury shrugs his shoulders, "He (Payson coach Dan Lunt) says he's beaten us once. He may have, but I don't remember it."

Even though the series is one-sided, this has turned into a rivalry. If there is one team Payson would love to beat, it's these Bulldogs.

Just minutes before tip-off, while the team gathers in the locker room, Schoonover tells the team of a conversation he had with the officials after the JV game was over.

"The referees before the game heard Dan Lunt talking (in the locker room). They asked me what he (Lunt) has against Provo. He heard them telling his (varsity) players, "I hate Provo. We're got to kill them. I'm sick of them coming in here and winning," Schoonover said. "They're going to be fired up and come after you. It will be a challenge."

Drury chips in, "It's fun that they hate us."

The stage has been set. Provo's vision is focused. Provo always seems to be geared up to play Payson. The Bulldogs know they own Payson and they revel in that fact.

Payson comes with a new defensive wrinkle. Lunt assigns scrappy guard Daniel Tervort to shadow Hagen. He denies Hagen the ball, full-court pressure, he mirrors his every move. Drury, with a bold

Provo players wait in the hall minutes before tipoff. One of the traditions before the game is to slap the "Play like a Champion Wall."

move, tells Stringham he is now the point guard, despite being a forward and having never practiced the point all season.

Drury's move works. Stringham brings the ball up court. Lunt's move works as well.

Tervort smothers Hagen. He seldom touches the ball, but hits a three-pointer in the first and second quarter. His second-quarter shot gives Provo a 21-13 lead.

After Tai Wesley scores to give Provo a 28-17 lead, Lunt screams at the official.

"You're intimidated by Provo!"

The official returns the fire.

"Don't go there."

Provo takes a 31-21 lead at the half.

In the locker room Drury writes a name on the board and puts an asterisk by it.

*Tika Wesley.

"Cory, I'm not going to play you in any more JV games if you want to shoot every time you touch the ball," Drury says.

Carter hit one three-pointer, but also took a quick ill-timed three-pointer that missed.

"If you're open take a shot, but don't be in a hurry to shoot. There's the guy—Tika," Drury said. "They're angry. They're 0-2 in the region. They're desperate. I respect them for what they're doing. If we were 0-2, we'd be doing that too, but if we get the ball inside to our big guys, the game will be over. After we did that a few times in the first half, what happened? It opened it up for our threes. But then we thought we should only shoot threes."

Payson's leading scorer, Walynn Burgess, picks up his fourth foul just 30 seconds into the third quarter. Provo goes to Tika, who delivers 10 second-half points.

Tika taps the ball loose and Stringham picks it up at the free-throw line and races down court to lay in a finger roll over two Payson defenders, one of the more athletic plays of the year. Stringham's play put Provo up 48-31. The Bulldogs are playing as well as they have all year.

Midway through the fourth quarter, Hagen takes over the point guard duties and hits four straight free throws.

Schoonover reminds Drury to put in Mercer with 18 seconds left. Steve Torkildson also checks in and hits a three-pointer at the buzzer to cap off a 60-45 win in the Lions Den.

"I think one of the reasons why we have their number is they don't have a philosophy on how to play us," Drury says. "They try to beat us a different way each time we play them."

In the locker room, Drury is grinning. These are the wins that makes the time in the summer seem worth it. It's wins like these that answer the annual question that a coach often asks himself. "Is all this headache worth it?

"Fellas, I want to thank you for allowing me to coach one of the funnest games I've ever coached," Drury said. "I've coached this game a lot of years. Every time I see a new challenge. I love it."

※※※

The first round of region play ends with a home game against an intriguing American Fork team. American Fork already figured to be a region title contender before the team agreed to accept the transfer of 6'-11", senior center Stephan Zimmerman, who signed to play for Rick Majerus at the University of Utah.

American Fork returns three starters off last year's team plus Zimmerman, who was unhappy at Mountain View and for the third time in his high school career, transferred to another school in Utah County.

Zimmerman had checked out Provo in his search for other schools, but didn't feel like it was a good fit, so he ended up at American Fork.

Logically, American Fork was due to upset somebody, perhaps Provo.

Provo's offense erupts for 17 first-quarter points as the Bulldogs pound the ball inside to Tai for eight points and Tika for six points.

But in the second quarter, the Bulldogs get away from what is working and once again the offense stalls. The only basket of the quarter is a bucket inside from Tika.

In the locker room Drury erupts. The energy in his voice is evident. He's not shouting, but he is louder than usual.

Point guard Kade Koop gets the team into its offense. By the end of the season, Koop emerged as one of the team's top players.

On the board he writes "Lazy."

"You are so damn lazy. You're about as lazy of a team as you can be. Tika, you're probably the worst one. We haven't had a four-pass possession. I'm really disappointed with the inside players.

"You're so damn lazy, you want THIS GAME TO COME ALONG SO EASY.

"Joey (scoreless in the first half on 0-1 shooting) you've lost your starting job. You'll have to prove to me you can play off the bench.

"And Mick, you're damn close to losing your job. This team wants to beat you. You scored two points in the second quarter. I'm 51 years old and I think I could go out there and score two points. In fact, I know I could.

"You were told by the papers that you were a good team and you believed it. Work, that's how you've gotten here, but you don't want to work.

"Scott, it was fun to watch you play hard. You were only in for five or six possessions, but you played hard.

"Coach (Lobendahn), who am I starting on the guard line for Joey?"

"Corey."

Carter starts the second half. Pututau comes in with 5:56 left in the quarter and quickly responds by hitting a three-pointer to give Provo a 26-22 lead.

The Bulldogs take a 30-28 lead into the fourth quarter where they finally open up some breathing room.

Zimmerman scores to open the fourth quarter and tie the game at 30. But an intentional foul is called on American Fork when Tika tries to go up for a shot in the key. A technical foul is then called on American Fork coach Doug Meacham, who didn't like the call, and another technical is called on American Fork's bench.

Provo hits four of the six free throws and Tika then scores again, to make it a six-point swing. The Bulldogs then put the game away from the free-throw line. Hagen hits six straight. Kade Koop comes off the bench and comes up with a steal and is fouled. He hits both free throws. Tai Wesley and Stringham each hit free throws to help Provo win 51-39.

Zimmerman leads American Fork with 21 points, but despite his presence along with that of 6'8" Taylor Brown, Provo has success inside.

Tai finishes with 16 points. Tika has 14 and Hagen has 12, including 9 of 10 free throws.After the game Drury says he's pleased with about eight minutes of their game and reiterates the season-long game plan.

He writes on the board: Pound the Ball.

"With the personnel I'm playing we need to pound the ball in there. Earlier in the year when we were pounding the ball inside, where were half of our shots coming from?"

Drury answers his own question.

"Outside."

"When we pound the ball, they have to help. You're not as good of a team as you were two weeks ago, because you let down," Drury tells the team in the locker room. "Tai's coming on for us, but he's still not the man. You're the man (Tika). You make the best decisions. We're 4-1 through the first round. Timpview is not going to go undefeated. We're going to beat those guys.

"Kade, I thought you came in and did a good job defensively. I may not need you as much next week. I might need Corbin, but good job."

Drury is done talking and the team files out of the team room and into the locker room where Snarr yells, "Scrub Cup!"

Announcement: Joey lost his starting job.

There is a mixed reaction. A few yeahs and a few boos.

Now for the nominees.

Tika fouls out on a blocking foul.

Drury moves his hips like he's Elvis trying to explain to the officials that it was a charge.

Lobendahn for wanting to sub Carter in for Tai when Provo needed another big man.

The winner is…

It's a tie.

Snarr can't decide, so he has a cup for both Mercer and Stringham. Neither one had been verbally acknowledged with a nomination, but The Scrub Cup President has power to do this.

"I looked at Corbin when he was out there in the fourth quarter and he was picking a zit on his chest.

"And then there was Craig. When the technical was called, he stepped up like he was going to shoot the free throws instead of Mick."

The speeches are short. There's a dance to get to and for the first time this year, Provo practiced on a Saturday. Drury put in a new play, one that he would call "Wilson" after a former assistant coach.

The play is a cross court pass with a high post screen designed to get Provo's point guard an open three-point shot.

On Monday, Drury uses the last part of practice to have fun. The first half of region play is over and there is just three more weeks left in the season. It's time to break up the monotony, so Drury offers a Provo Bulldogs sweatshirt as a prize.

Schoonover laughs. It's not a $700 jersey like the one LaBron James got.

Drury calls the team together and explains the rules. Everyone split up and shoot 10 free throws and everyone comes back and report how many you made. Those with the worst percentage will shoot one-and-one first. Those with the best scores shoot last.

Stringham, Tyson Hindee, and Dustin Migliaccio all hit two in a row and advance. Eric Walker misses to end the streak. After Mercer, Pututau, Kade Koop, and Jordan Snarr hit two in a row, Tika, Scott Ady, and Garrett Groesbeck miss.

Drury adds a provision. If you've missed, you can go down to one of the other baskets, make seven in a row and comeback, and if you do that before everyone is done shooting, you can get back in.

In a minute Groesbeck and Ady are back. Tika and Walker join them. It looks like this will go on forever, but after 20 minutes the competition is down to just Hagen and Snarr.

The team roots for the underdog. As Hagen gets ready to shoot, the players, who are all lined up in the key, start a wave with their arms and yell.

HEY! AHHHHHH!

Swish.

Snarr's turn.

Sssh. There's quiet.

Swish.

Hagen steps up for another shot.

Hey! Whiz kid. Hey!

Swish.

Snarr answers.

Finally, Snarr leaves it short.

Hagen can now win.

The screams get louder. A ball is thrown in the air to try and distract him, but Hagen is money.

Swish, game over.

Being the good friend that he is, Ady accepts the sweatshirt and puts it on.

"It looks better on me."

The Bulldogs are now ready for the second round, starting with a game at Spanish Fork.

"You've got to loosen it up a little and have some fun," Drury says of the practice. "At this point in the season, you have to have some fun."

It's no surprise that Provo is 4-1 and is still in the hunt for a region title. It seems consistency is Provo's trademark. The Bulldogs rarely lose to a team they are supposed to beat.

But as predictable as the first half of region play was, it fails to compare what will happen over the next four weeks.

CHAPTER FOURTEEN

A SPANISH FORK SURPRISE

Just minutes after Provo opened the second round of region play with a big road win at Spanish Fork, beating the Dons for the second time this season, the team filed into the visiting locker room, where Drury had a little surprise waiting for them.

A scolding lecture.

"I'm not happy with you. I don't want to be skipping because we got a win. I don't understand you. You play three possessions where you step up and kick their ass, then you go right back to your passivity. I don't understand you."

Drury believes there are two times during the year when he can rip his team. Any more than two can be detrimental. If he doesn't do it, the team may get complacent.

"Their coach was almost begging me before the game not to beat them by 20. He said (before the game) our kids need to be in the game," Drury said. "They knew they couldn't beat you, and you let them play within 10 points of you. You can't be happy if your objective is to be a state champion."

Drury continues to drive his point home by talking about Timpview.

"You've gotten to be like our football team. You can't beat them (Timpview) because you don't scrap. You're going to beat Springville. They already have their baseball bats out. They're talking to each other before the game and saying 'I wish we could take live pitching instead of hitting off that machine.' You'll beat them, but you won't beat them 91-29 (like Timpview) because you don't have a killer instinct in you.

"I never thought in my coaching life that I'd say that. You won't beat them if you play like that. The best offensive player in the league is Pinegar and the best defensive player of the year is Miles. Everywhere I go people are telling me, 'Pinegar just chewed us up and Miles is so good.'

"I'd say we had 50 possessions and I'd say we played hard on 10-12 of those. I'd be doing a disservice to you if I said nice job. Way to beat a terrible team by 10."

Now remember, the sweat on the team's forehead is still there. They are just minutes removed from a 49-39 win.

Why is Drury so upset?

Because the team is not playing with a purpose. If there is one thing that stews inside a coach's gut more than bad chili, it's under-achieving. Playing below your potential.

"Mick, you've got to be aggressive. Your mediocre is better than most point guards' best game. You've got to get rid of that noncha-lant, acting too cool to play attitude. You're not going to beat good teams playing like that," Drury says. "You won't beat an Olympus or Highland, they scrap too much. That's why they are ahead of East. East is a better team. You've got to get more hustle. I'd like to bottle one fifth of Corbin's aggressiveness and give it to you (Mick)."

After Drury unleashes his frustration, he passes out a compliment to Pututau.

"Joey, that's the best you've played in a while. You've got to keep that up."

Fortunately for Provo, Pututau turned in one of his best perform-ances of the season and if anyone needed a big game, it was Pututau. The pressure on him was mounting. He'd scored just three points in the team's last two games, but against Spanish Fork he came out fir-ing.

Provo started the game with back-to-back baskets from Tika. The Bulldogs then ran the play called "Wilson."

"Wilson," Drury called out.

Pututau hit a three and just like that Provo was up 7-0 and Spanish Fork coach Rex Brimhall called a timeout.

Provo fans jumped all over Brimhall, who wanted a charging call on Tika.

"Rex needs his bottle, Rex needs his bottle," the Provo fans chanted.

The Dons battle back to cut the lead to 16-10 at the end of the first quarter.

A group of Spanish Fork girls did their best to distract Provo. Hey, why not try something different? Why not try a little psychological warfare? The Dons were desperate for a win.

Brimhall hasn't beaten Provo, and his predecessor Mike Gardner, never beat Provo either.

One of the signs the girls held up said, "Wesley your skin is as soft as butta."

Two other signs were aimed at Hagen. "No. 11, you're my dream boat."

"No. 11, you rock my world."

It's one thing to scream, stomp on the benches, blow horns, and pound a drum, but there just may be some logic to this new method—attractive girls hitting on the players during the game. Brilliant!

Spanish Fork junior guard Jordan Daley hit a pair of three pointers to help cut the lead to 16-15, but Tika answered with five straight points to help Provo take a 22-17 lead into the locker room.

"22 points with the tempo like this? We should have 35 points don't you think?" Drury said as he bounced around from topic to topic at half time.

"Mick I can't believe you're 0-6 and 1-2 from the free-throw line. If you're going to shoot like that I want that sweater back (from winning a free-throw shooting contest in practice). I'll give it to (Jordan) Snarr."

Drury continues, "We've got to come up with balls that are loose. They're having too much fun on offense. We're only up five and we should be up 10, 12 or 14 points."

The second half begins on a light note. Brimhall calls over to Drury. He holds up a baby's bottle that's half filled with milk.

"They (pointing to the Provo fans) said I needed it," Brimhall said.

Provo came out fired up. Tika scored off an offensive rebound basket and Hagen hit a three-pointer to put Provo up 27-17, but the Bulldogs couldn't put Spanish Fork away.

Gavin Gardner drilled a three-pointer, and Daley popped another three to trim the lead to 29-26, but Pututau answered. He hit a jumper then came up with a steal and fed Stringham, but Stringham missed a dunk. Pututau got the rebound and scored to give Provo a 33-26 lead at the end of the third quarter.

Pututau hit a three-pointer to start the fourth quarter, but then disaster happened when Tika and Spanish Fork's Bryce Dodge scuffled and fell to the floor for a rebound. Tika was called for his fourth foul as the officials quickly separated the two.

Dodge then took a fall at the other end of the court, flopping to the floor and drawing a whistle. Mission accomplished. Tika had fouled out of the game.

"He actually apologized. He told me, 'You've got to do what you've got to do,'" Tika said.

Provo's lead dwindled to 36-33 with 3:39 left in the game after Gardner hit one of two free throws, but the Bulldogs finally pulled away. Hagen zipped a pass to Stringham under the basket for a layup. After a Spanish Fork turnover, Pututau hit a three-pointer and Hagen sank two free throws to open up a 43-33 lead.

With 16 seconds left in the game, Drury turned to coach Green and said, "I want a sophomore (to reward the way the team has been playing). Who do you want, Tyler Miller?"

Green nods in acceptance.

Eric Walker also checks in.

"You got that?" He asks a newspaper reporter after the game. "I got in for 3.4 seconds," he says with a proud laugh.

Pututau finished with 13 points, seven rebounds, four assists, and four steals. Despite fouling out in the first minute of the fourth quarter, Tika finished with 21 points and six rebounds. A coach from Snow College talked to Tika after the game.

The players are happy with the win, but the coaches are still in a foul mood. Coach Keli announces "No singing" on the bus ride home.

Lobendahn strums his ukulele and sings to himself, while the players announce "Scrub Cup!"

The nominees are Tika for fouling out and Tika and Steve Torkildson for getting blocked while going up for dunks. Stringham also missed a chance for a dunk. Once again Stringham adds to his collection.

Speech, speech.

"I felt really stupid missing the dunk," Stringham says.

It's a short speech, but it's a short bus ride.

After the bus pulls in, Drury takes Kade Koop into his office and tells him why he took him out after missing the front end of a one-and-one.

"It's like a rookie facing a guy throwing heat who strikes out on three straight pitches," Drury said. "You don't let him hit again. You don't put him in the position to fail."

※※※

If there was a game junior forward Dustin Migliaccio figured to get in, it was Provo's rematch with Springville, the Region 6 bottom dweller.

But the junior varsity game is underway and Migliaccio is in jeans and he's wearing a black t-shirt. He's not hobbling like he's injured and it isn't a problem with grades.

Migliaccio has made a decision. He quit the team.

"I just felt like my future was in baseball," Migliaccio explained.

The baseball season is still a month away, but Migliaccio wanted to miss three practices to play in a tournament in southern Utah with some friends.

Drury told him no and Migliaccio didn't like the answer, so he made the decision to give up basketball.

The team is surprised and disappointed by Migliaccio's decision, but it isn't much of a distraction.

Springville played Provo tough in the first meeting. The goal this time for the Bulldogs is to improve. Lobendahn wants 80 points.

It's been a week since the team's last game and the practices leading up to the game have been some of the best all year. It quickly shows.

Provo starts off the game with a 17-2 run. Joey hits his first four 3-pointers, four of those come in the first quarter as the Bulldogs blow open to a 26-7 at the end of the quarter.

At the half, Provo extends the lead to 44-23 and in the locker room Drury tells them not to settle.

"You're up 21. Do you want to beat this team by 21 points? I hope not," Drury says. "Don't do that to yourself."

Another Pututau three-pointer gives Provo a 54-29 lead with 4:25 left in the third quarter as the Bulldogs continue to cruise. Finally, the blow out Torkildson and Ady have been waiting for. Now it's time for their reward—quality minutes. Eric Walker, Tyler Miller, and Snarr all check in with over a minute to play.

The final score is 81-46.

The team finishes with a whopping 20 steals. Tika leads the way with five. Stringham and Mercer each have four steals.

The only downer on the night is the team's free-throw performance. Provo shoots just 14 of 30.

Zac Erekson is one of the highlights for Springville in a miserable season for first-year coach Brent Knapp. Erekson finishes with 16 points.

After the game Drury says that had the team made free throws, they could have scored 100 points. He then writes three schools on the board, Payson, Timpview, and American Fork.

"I'm happy with this game, but I'm not elated," Drury said. "There it is right there (pointing to the board)."

Three tough teams left before the state tournament.

The win caps off an emotional day for Schoonover, who passed a kidney stone the night before the game and gave an emotional speech after the game.

"You guys are like family. We care about you," he says trying to hold back the tears. "We've worked our butts off to make this fun for you."

Provo finally played the way it was capable of. The Bulldogs didn't play down to the level of their competition and with three games left in the regular season, the team's peak performance came just in time, because when the team returned for practice on Monday, Drury would have some bad news.

※※※

It's a Monday afternoon, a day before the Bulldogs are to host Payson and the team usually filters in the gym and shoots until practice begins, but on this day, they are told to sit down on the bleachers. Drury never starts practice like this.

Looking around, the players notice, one player is missing. Forward Scott Ady is no where to be found.

On Saturday Ady went roller skating with Pututau and Hagen and their dates. While Ady was skating around the oval, he turned his knee in an awkward position and went down in severe pain.

It's not official yet, there are more tests to take, but Ady is out for the year.

After Ady went down, he was taken to Hagen's house. Still in severe pain, they decided to call Donnie Bills, the school's trainer.

Never mind the fact that it's midnight. When someone's hurt, the players know Bills is the person to call. He is their crutch. When Koop took prescription pain pills in Hawaii and the coaches weren't sure what to do, they called Bills. And now with Ady hurt and not knowing how his insurance, which is in Canada, would cover any expenses, they hoped Bills would know what to do.

Bills rushes over to Hagen's house to check Ady out. He ices the knee and calls a doctor to report what he sees. He gets a prescription for the pain and goes to the pharmacy to pick it up and deliver it to Ady.

Now that's not in Bills' job description, but he's never been one to be limited by his job description. Bills graduated from BYU (1992) physical education, emphasis on sports medicine and worked at Granite High School for a year and then moved to physical therapy and physician assistant.

When he was an intern at Orem High School, he loved working at the high school so much and never had a better learning experience. When he was told to end his relationship at the high school and move on to work with BYU intramurals, Bills declined. He lost his scholarship over the issue, but felt it was worth it.

On a whim Bills stopped by Provo High to see if they had an opening in the future. It turned out that Provo's trainer had just quit the same day he'd stopped by.

A few days later, Provo asked him the question, "When can you start?"

He asked, "When do you need me?"

"Today."

Bills started the next day and has been a stabilizing influence ever since, providing education for students and a valuable resource to the school and to parents and students.

"I think I'm saving them a lot of money. I can do the things they can at therapy. Let's say someone has a major ankle sprain. I can say this does need to get x-rayed or this does not. A parent might say they're going in no matter what."

One of the first injuries Bills dealt with was one he'll never forget.

"The first year I was there, a football player had a brain injury," Bills said. "He complained of headache and kept saying his eye felt like it was going to explode and his eyes were dilated. I asked him if he felt nauseous and he kind of got mad at me and said 'no.' He then threw up all over me."

Bills knew he had a problem and within minutes an ambulance was on the field.

"I don't know if I saved his life, but I did what I was trained to do in that situation. He had bleeding on the brain, a subdural hemotoma. The doctor told me he's lucky to be alive."

The player is now wheelchair bound and has little upper body movement and at times has trouble doing anything for himself, but the incident is another testimonial on why Bills' job is invaluable.

On most days Bills says he treats about 10 athletes a day, a little more during football season. He also works with three to five athletes a day that would would require a session of physical therapy if he weren't around, but most are saved the expense since they know Bills can work with them until they are ready to suit up again.

After a trial period, Drury has come to trust in Bills' expertise, even if it took awhile for Drury to warmup to the idea.

"He told me not to baby his athletes and that I had to earn his trust," Bills explained. "He was stern with me, but I think there was a stage where he wanted me to prove to him that I knew what I was doing."

Seven years later, Bills has earned Drury's trust and now talks of expansion. He's trying to get more space, more room for physical therapy. He wants to make Provo the envy of the other high schools. He simply wants to get the athletic training program at the same level as the basketball program.

"Time is the biggest issue I have with the program. I don't really have the time to dedicate myself to just rehab. I've got to get players ready for practice."

Now Bills has a project. Just when it looked like Ady would be able to give Provo some significant minutes, Ady's injury has proven painful in more ways than one.

"Scott was helping us. He played well against Payson and gave us some good minutes against Springville," Drury told his team. "Now you'll have to step it up."

CHAPTER FIFTEEN

IT'S OK TO REMEMBER

All the interviews are done. The players are long gone. They've either all gone out to eat, paired up with some girls, or gone home.

Only a few custodians remain to clean up after the game.

Without a lot of fouls called, the game went by fast. If I leave now I can still get home at a decent time.

But as I walk toward the exit, something catches my eye. I look up on the wall and see a glass case that hangs on the wall. Enclosed in the case are two green jerseys—No. 4 and No. 45—the only Provo jerseys to be retired in the school's 91-year history.

I wonder as fans pass by the memorial every game if anyone remembers David Liddiard and R.J. Staheli. I wonder what they would be doing now. I wonder if they would show up to watch practice like many of the other former players and visit with Drury.

I knew David Liddiard and R.J. Staheli. I covered them. I interviewed them when they played at Provo High and tonight their memory won't let me go home.

I must stop and reflect. Usually, I'm like everyone else. I pass by the encased memorial without a second thought, but tonight is different. Tonight I don't want to leave, I just want to reflect, but while I do I wonder if it's okay to remember or if by writing this it will just dig up painful memories.

The year was 1993, when Liddiard and Staheli were seniors on Provo's basketball team. I approached Drury about an idea I had for an article for the newspaper.

I wondered what it would be like to follow the team around as they prepared for the state tournament? What does he tell the team in the locker room and during the timeouts? What is the bus ride home like when you win or lose? What do I miss out on when I sit by the scorers table and not by the bench?

Drury allowed me an all-access pass. So I went to every practice. I was in the huddle during timeouts, I was in the locker room when Drury went over his pre-game preparation and in the locker room after the game to see how the team would handle a win or a loss with the pressures of the state tournament. I even found a spot on the bus and rode to and from each game as the team made a push for another title.

Provo didn't win the state championship in the 1993 season, but the Bulldogs did finish second in Region 4 and qualified for the state tournament. The Bulldogs beat Hillcrest in the first round of the tournament and finished with a 13-9 overall record.

For Provo it was an average year with two remarkable seniors.

David Liddiard and R.J. Staheli.

One day in his office, I reflected with Drury on the memories he had of Liddiard.

"David dominated the game at the hardest possible position, the wing," Drury said. "I remember one time he literally hurdled a guy who was 6'4". He faked out a guy and drove the baseline where (Timpview's) Nate Cooper was waiting to take a charge, and he hurdled him and dunked it. I turned to my assistant coach and said, 'You're coaching the rest of the game. I'm done.' I've never seen a high school player do that."

After a pause Drury looked down for a minute and then returned his focus to my eyes.

"I've never been closer to a player than I was with David," he said.

And he would never get that close to another player again.

A number of people were close to David, including his nephew Steven, who was just seven months younger than David.

"He was the best friend I've ever had. He was a really talented player. He ran a 4.4/40 and he could jump out of the gym for being a white guy," said Steve Liddiard. "I went to Mountain View (high school) my sophomore year, but then our family moved right behind David's family and I went to Provo. I played basketball mainly so I could be around him. We would play one-on-one all the time."

David was the youngest of eight children. He was the caboose of the family, by a whopping five years. He quickly became the apple of the family's eye and in high school was the kind of person that his peers respected.

"In high school it seemed like the popular people all had money," said former teammate Chris Strong. "Me and Dave came from the wrong side of the tracks if you will. Dave was friendly to everyone, to the popular people and to the handicapped people. Dave never got caught up in the idea that he had to hang out with the popular crowd. He hung out with the people he wanted to hang out with."

He was also a player that his teammates respected on the court. He was 6'-3", but he played bigger. He could drive hard to the basket or pull up and pop a three-pointer. He could fly inside for an offensive rebound or he could sneak inside to help a teammate and block a shot.

"I remember when we were playing in the state tournament. He (David) came out of the game with a dislocated finger," said former teammate B.J. Chandler. "I could see his bone. His finger wasn't pointing in the right direction. He just taped up his finger and went back in. I had a lot of respect for him before, but after that my respect for him peaked."

Liddiard averaged close to 20 points and eight rebounds in his senior year and was named First-Team All-State by the *Salt Lake Tribune,* but his size left him labeled a tweener. He was in-between a guard and a forward. Division I teams felt he was too small to play forward at that level, so he opted to play at Snow College, where he could prove Division I coaches wrong.

Snow College coach Jon Judkins knew he had a coupe.

"David started for me. He was probably the most highly recruited freshman that I've ever coached. Everyone wanted Dave. He went on a (two-year church) mission and I thought I wouldn't get him back. I know BYU talked to him, but he wanted to come back. He was very special. He had a big future in basketball."

It took Judkins just two weeks to realize all the hype was true. After watching Liddiard practice for two weeks he asked himself, "How in the world did I get this player?"

The Liddiard family could ask themselves the same question. He was born five years after his parents thought they were done having children, so not only was he the baby, he was pampered.

Staheli was a 6'7" forward, short on athletic ability, but tall on integrity and work ethic. He didn't look like a basketball player. Chandler called him the "Undercover Hoopster."

"I remember thinking in my mind that every time I went up against him in practice, I was going to work him (R.J.)," Chandler said. "He doesn't look like a basketball player. By looking at him you'd think he should be playing chess or Nintendo or thumb wars, but whenever I played against him, I was the one that got worked. He was quiet but strong. He was a great teammate."

It's easy for former teammates to come up with stories on their friends. Strong recalled the time the two were involved in an assembly.

"I remember one time R.J. and I were in the best legs contest. There was a sheet up over us so you couldn't see who was who. There's no way he had better legs than I did, but I think people figured out it was him and voted for him," he said. "Coach Drury used to say 4-6-12 all the time. Four hours a day, six days a week, 12 months a year. David and R.J. took it to heart."

R.J. was one of four children of Ron and Jan Staheli. He was a member of the National Honor Society.

RJ's brother Joel wore No. 45 when Provo won the title in 1997.

R.J. wasn't as athletic as Liddiard, but he made up for it in other ways. He once made 78 free throws in a row during a practice.

Staheli and Liddiard decided to spend a weekend together with some other friends at Bear Lake in northern Utah. But before the friends took off for their weekend trip, Liddiard had a stop to make.

What, did he forget the ice?

His fishing pole?

The cooler?

Nope, Liddiard's stop was to see his niece, who was laying in a hospital bed. His fun weekend could wait.

They spent the weekend at Bear Lake. Liddiard and Staheli were with three other friends Darin Garner, Greg Biddulph, and Michael Paulos. All five friends had recently returned from two-year missions for The Church of Jesus Christ of Latter-day Saints.

They had to cut the weekend short because they had planned on coming back Sunday morning to attend a church service. They left early on a Sunday morning on September 8, 1996 to attend a church meeting where their longtime friend and former teammate. Chris Strong was returning from a church mission in Philadelphia. He'd only been home for five days and hadn't yet seen his friends.

Liddiard was driving a 1992 Pontiac Grand Prix, and his four friends piled in. They were running a little behind, but no matter. The roads were practically deserted on Sunday morning at 8 a.m.

They were near a small town called Willard, about an hour away from Provo, when disaster happened about 8:45 a.m.

The police estimate Liddiard was going about 90 mph when he must have looked away for a split second or perhaps fatigue caused him to lose control of the car on a slight curve in the road. The car hit an embankment and rolled several times. Liddiard and Staheli were sitting in the front seat, wearing seat belts.

The other three were in the back and were not wearing seat belts. Biddulph was thrown from the vehicle and somehow ended up underneath the car.

He was taken to the hospital with a head injury, broken bones, and facial cuts. He was listed in "very critical condition" as doctors tried to repair the internal damage.

Paulos escaped the accident in the best shape. He was listed in critical condition and eventually got out of the hospital as did Biddulph.

But Liddiard, Staheli, and Garner did not. They received substantial head injuries and were rushed to a local hospital where they were declared dead.

Ron Staheli, R.J's father, was a bishop in the LDS Church at the time. He was in a church meeting when he was called out and told there had been an accident and three boys were dead. He was told his boy R.J. was in critical condition.

Ron's reply?

Thank you, God?

No.

This was his response.

"I think you've made a mistake, my son is dead."

Somehow Ron already knew. There was a mixup. R.J. was dead.

Word of the tragedy spread fast.

"I remember standing there speaking to the whole audience and they were crying and I didn't know why," Strong said. "I thought my brother had died. It took me about five minutes after the meeting was over to figure out what happened."

Many of the people who came to hear Strong speak were also friends of David and the news broke just before the meeting began, leaving those in attendance stunned with silence.

Regardless of where they were when the news broke, it didn't come any easier.

"I was on my mission (Spokane, Washington) the day it happened. I spoke in church that day and when we got back to our apartment there was a message on the machine from home," Steve Liddiard said. "I knew we weren't supposed to get calls from home, so I ignored it. When we got back later that night there was another message, an emergency message to call home. When I called, my dad choked up when he told me David had died in a car accident. I remember yelling, 'Nooooo! It can't be. How did it happen?'"

Life had just changed dramatically. Nothing would ever be quite the same. Life's taste buds had just been numbed.

"I had a hard time sleeping for the rest of my mission. It took some of the drive away from my mission," Steve said. "I still did well and it helped me when I was teaching, because I would tear up almost every time I would teach."

Steve didn't come home for the funeral. The family thought it was best he stay on his mission and concentrate on his church work, but everything would be much more difficult.

"It was tough to come home and even go in our backyard. It was like a ghost town. Our families shared the same back yard. It was hard for me to go to Provo High games," Steve said. "After he died, I wasn't as into it (basketball)."

Still, Steve Liddiard continued his basketball career. He was a prototypical power forward, even though he's undersized (6'4") he was strong. He played a year at Snow College and one at Utah Valley State College before finishing up at Division II Southern Colorado.

Even now, after years have passed by, it's hard to think about the size of the footprints they have left behind.

"When I look back on it, it was a shock to me. I remember that I was sad, but I didn't cry," Strong added. "Later when I visited David's mother and we began sharing stories, then I broke down and cried. It was a lot more comforting for me to know that both completed the task they were asked to do here on earth."

To look back on what happened is just like viewing something in your rearview mirror. Memories that appear in the mirror are closer (to the heart) than they appear.

"Time changes a lot of things. I can think about memories without getting choked up all the time. There hasn't been a day that goes by without thinking about him," Steve added. "I've come to the understanding that he's gone. Because of my beliefs of myself and my family that we'll see him again, that's made it easier to handle."

Speaking for David's 20 nieces and nephews, Steve said, "The memories are still there, they'll never go away. It just won't be as difficult to handle. We're just waiting for the day when we can throw our arms around him again."

Like many members of The Church of Jesus Christ of Latter-day Saints, both Liddiard and Staheli served church missions when they turned 19. Staheli went to Cape Town, South Africa and Liddiard to the Philippines.

Both nearly died while on their missions.

Staheli was riding a bike and was hit. He was in a coma and given up for dead when miraculously he came out of the coma.

The family had come to grips that R.J. was gone for good. In fact, R.J.'s mother went to Africa to get the body, but miraculously, he came out of his coma. He came home to recover, then went back.

Liddiard was bitten by a dog and had to undergo a series of rabies shots, but that was nothing compared to the time he was bit by a poisonous snake.

The families believe their sons were called on another mission.

"We just felt like they all died together for a reason," said Darin's father, Ron Gardner. "That's the way the Lord wanted it. They still have a mission to accomplish, but in a different place."

Elder Jeffery R. Holland, a member of the Quorum of the Twelve Apostles for the The Church of Jesus Christ of Latter-day Saints, attended Staheli's funeral and gave the family some words of comfort.

"This is a very sobering occasion, but it is not a tragic occasion . . . Tragedies have unhappy endings. This one has a very, very happy ending."

Happy ending? That comment needed an explanation.

The family explained why there was a reason for hope. The reason the stories of these young men end on a happy note is they were all people who did things for others while trying to deflect credit for their good deeds away from themselves.

David's sister, Cathy Page said, "David was our golden boy," as she wiped away her tears. "It was no secret that he was our favorite . . . He knew he was adored, but he couldn't understand why."

Ron Staheli, R.J's father, gave an example of his son's attitude. "There I was waiting to be picked up outside the mall on Christmas Eve," he said. "My ride was late and I was growing impatient. Then I saw R.J., who was late because of a miscommunication, coming over to me with a big smile and he put his big arms around me. Any feelings of discontent quickly went away as I was affected by his smile and his good nature…R.J. was our gentle giant."

Many of David and R.J.'s friends and classmates got together in June for their 10-year high school reunion.

Strong was in town, having just finished his MBA from Harvard. He said one of the activities during the reunion was to take timeout and write in a card for each member of the class of 1993 that had passed away. The cards would be delivered to the family of those who had died.

At Snow College, about two hours south of Provo, the wake of David Liddiard and R.J. Staheli's impact is still being felt.

"We named our Inspirational Award, our most important award, the Liddiard/Staheli award. It goes to our most inspirational player. We engraved their faces on a wood plaque to honor them," Judkins said. "Everyone asks about it. I still think about it a ton. They meant so much to our program."

Snow dedicated the season to the two players and retired their uniforms for two years.

"One thing I always think about is if people remember," Steve Liddiard said. "I wonder if people remember what he and R.J. were like. Both of them were the type of people who would do anything they could to help someone out. They always tried to do what was right.

"I just wonder if people remember them or if it's just a plaque on the wall."

Me too.

Maybe there will be nights at Snow College when someone will be drawn to a picture of the Liddiard/Staheli award and pause, then wonder what they could have done, what they might have been or then again, what they're doing now.

I've come to realize that it's okay to remember. It's okay to let them know that we still think of them and that if there was a universal consensus, some cosmic poll taken, the results would hardly be a mystery. The fact is they are loved and missed and the numbers coming from the exit polls seem to be growing.

Even though time has taken them further way and has widened the road of our recall, there is still a memorial that's enclosed in a glass case that players pass by each game. Most of the times they don't stop to reflect. But once in a while, a player, a parent, or a sportswriter will hear the silent call that comes from the memorial.

And what does it say?

A different message for everyone.

On this night, the message is: When you live your life the right way, you never really leave at all. Your impact echoes on and on and on and on and on and on and on.

CHAPTER SIXTEEN

THE PROPHET JEREMIAH

The butterflies are racing through Corbin Mercer's stomach. He's not sure what to do. He has already drafted a letter, a note, with his co-author, Craig Stringham.

"Dear Miss Beautiful. The only reason I would go to Payson is to see you." The note was signed Corbin and Craig with their phone numbers.

They identify their target, a Payson cheerleader, who just happens to be Payson coach Dan Lunt's daughter.

Corbin finally gets up the courage to give the note to her. He starts towards her but chickens out and turns around. She's cheering under the basket along the baseline, next to six other Payson cheerleaders.

Ah! This is tough.

Five minutes later there's a breakthrough. Mercer walks up behind her and taps her on the shoulder and hands her the note, then he walks out of the gym.

Mercer is not sure what to do next so he sends in teammates Steve Torkildson and Kade Koop to check her out and to see how she's reacting.

Torkildson and Koop soon leave to give Mercer an update. A few minutes later, Mercer is back. He sits on the benches and talks to Schooney. Occasionally, the cheerleader sneaks a peak at Mercer and smiles.

Meanwhile, Tika talks about busting out the old warmups from their sophomore year. Hagen shows up in the fourth quarter of the girls game, a fact that doesn't escape Drury.

The team is just minutes away from playing Payson. It's the

team's last home game of the season, but before the game Drury can sense the team is distracted. His instincts proved right.

In the locker room before the team takes the floor, Drury warns the team it's headed for a fall.

"You think you can just turn on the intensity (he flips the light switch and turns the lights off and back on). I went in the locker room and heard some of you talking about next year. You're going to get your asses kicked. You're out there sitting around a group of cheerleaders. I'm not very happy with your game preparations. You think that it's just Payson and that they're 2-5 and they're no good, but they're battling for a tournament spot. They have to win tonight. The way to get them down is to put your knee in their chest and pin them down early, in the first quarter, like you did against Springville. I hope you're ready to go, because Payson is ready."

Before the game, the parents of the seniors are honored. Each player is announced along with his parents. They meet at center court where the player gives his dad a hug, his mom a a kiss and a flower.

Stringham's mom gets the flower and says, "It's been 16 years since I started doing this, now this is my last one…"

After a slight pause she says, "I'm going to miss it."

Finally, it's tipoff and as Drury predicted, Provo isn't ready to play. Payson jumps out to a 10-4 lead on the strength of sophomore Tyler Newbold, who scores eight of the Lions' first 10 points.

The Bulldogs have just four points in the first six minutes. Drury then turns to the bench and says, "Just like I expected. They came out la dee dah, la dee dah, la dee dah."

Tika converts a three-point play to cut the lead to 12-11, but Payson's Walynn Burgess scores at the end of the quarter to help Payson to a 14-11 lead.

"We're way too passive. We're lucky to be down just three," Drury tells the team during the break between quarters.

Newbold adds five more points in the second quarter to help the Lions stay in control and take a 27-23 lead into the half.

The team knows it is playing poorly, especially on defense.

"I feel like taking the other coaches out and getting a burger," Drury says. "I feel like a prophet."

Coach Keli interjects "Jeremiah" and Drury comes back

with, "Yeah, the one no one listened to."

"We were right on the money about you guys screwing around and not being ready to play," Drury said. "These guys have to win. When you take the court you have to remember that.

"Give them credit. You've underestimated them. You are treating them like they're Springville, but this team has the best talent it's had in a long time. Their people think they have a team that is supposed to win the region. They've got to win. I can't tell you that enough. This is a state tournament game for them, you've got to play like it's a state tournament game to you."

After the scolding, Provo gets a basket from Tika to start the third quarter, but Newbold answers with a three-pointer. Pututau then scores and Hagen hits his only field goal of the night to cut the lead to 30-29. Tika then picks up a foul, reaching in against Burgess. The two knock heads and both players are left with a cut above the eye. Tika gets the worst of it, his gash keeps him out of the game while trainer Donnie Bills works to close the cut that will require ten stitches to close the wound.

Meanwhile, Brett Hiatt hits a three-pointer to give the Lions a 35-32 lead. Hagen hits one of two free throws to keep Provo within three at the end of the third quarter.

A Tai Wesley basket gives Provo its first lead of the game with 5:10 left in the game. Two minutes later Corey Carter hits the big shot of the game, a three-pointer, to give Provo a 42-38 lead with 2:10 to play.

Randy Beddes scores to cut the lead to 42-40 and Tai makes a good up and under move, but misses a layin with a minute left in the game, giving Payson a chance to tie the game.

Payson runs the clock down to 45 seconds and calls timeout. The Lions then look for a shot to tie the game. Payson point guard Daniel Tervort drives the baseline and dishes off to Burgess, who is inside the key, but Burgess isn't ready for the pass and fumbles the ball out of bounds.

Stringham is then fouled with nine seconds left. He makes one of two free throws, leaving Payson one more chance to tie the game.

The Lions call a timeout to set up a play with nine seconds to play. Drury tells his players the Bulldogs have a foul to give and to use it.

Tai does, but it nearly turns into a disaster. He grabs Tervort behind the three-point line just before Tervort shoots.

A foul is called and luckily it's ruled before the shot.

Drury drops his clipboard on the floor in disbelief, then calls a timeout. He wanted to use a foul, but not like that.

So now Payson tries again. The Lions get the ball to Beddes, Payson's 6'6" senior center, who takes a three-pointer at the top of the key, but misses. Pututau grabs the rebound and is fouled. He adds two free throws with two seconds left to give Provo a hard-fought 45-40 win.

Tika leads the team with 15 points, despite sitting out for half of the third and fourth quarter while getting his eye patched up.

Newbold's 18 points lead Payson, while Pututau turns in a strong game with 11 points and three steals. Hagen turns in one of his worst performances of the year. He has just three points and four turnovers.

In the locker room the team sits in the chairs and digs into a box of oranges. Drury grabs coach Keli's Thunderstruck poster, which has a picture of Timpview celebrating its win over Provo. He doesn't say a word, he just holds up the poster.

The only sound in the room is players peeling oranges. For nearly a minute not a word is spoken. Drury looks around the room at his players, while holding the poster. Finally, the silence is broken when he says, "Let's take a minute."

The Scrub Cup goes to Tai for shooting an air ball from 10-feet away. It's the weakest Scrub Cup of the year and some of the team don't feel up to it. They know they played so poorly, they don't feel like laughing and cheering.

As the players file out of the locker room, Drury calls Hagen into his office and tells him he needs him to concentrate on basketball only for the next two weeks.

"How we do in the state tournament is mainly going to be up to you. I'm not saying that if we lose it's your fault. The other guys are going to play here (he holds his hand up near his chin), they may fluctuate a little, but when you play well we win and when you don't play well we lose. That's a lot of pressure, but so what? You're the point guard."

Coach Keli, who is sitting on the couch, can't stay quiet anymore.

"I've heard that speech before, and that's a different version," he says.

The tone in his voice intensifies. "We win and you get the glory. We lose and you are the goat."

He then takes coach Schoonover's clipboard that is also used to draw up plays and snaps it half. "Do I make myself clear?"

Hagen nods and walks out of the office.

Schoonover is in the adjoining office calling in the results to the newspapers when Drury gets an idea. He takes the clipboard out of the garbage can and tapes it together with white tape, laughing while he tapes it together. The tape can't keep the clipboard from the obvious fact, that it's been broken, so Drury takes a piece of paper to cover cover the damage, while they wait to get a good laugh from Schoonover when he finds out what happened to his clipboard.

The next day, practice begins and there's no sign of Drury or Hagen. While the team warms up, Drury is talking to Hagen in his office.

When asked about his meeting, Drury says, "I can't tell you everything, we just had a talk about a few things."

When the practice is over, Drury smiles.

"That was one of his (Hagen's) best practices of the year."

And just in time. The rematch with Timpview is only a day away.

CHAPTER SEVENTEEN

TIMPVIEW, THE SEQUEL

It seems like everyone has a compliment for Timpview.

The T-Birds are a unanimous No. 1 and the question left to be asked is not whether Timpview will lose another game, but rather, can anyone give the T-Birds a game?

Before the game Spanish Fork coach Rex Brimhall talks about the teams in the region and has high praise for Timpview.

"That may be the best team I've ever seen in high school."

Provo's task is to snap Timpview's winning streak at the Thunderdome, Timpview's home court.

Gulp.

While the JV game is being played, Pututau and Hagen sit in the bleachers confident that for the first time since they were freshman, Provo will beat Timpview.

"They know last time we didn't play well until the final two minutes of the game and we still almost beat them," Hagen says. "I'm nervous, but not scared. I think they're scared. They're feeling it. The target is on their back."

Pututau says, "Our sources say they're losing sleep."

Sources?

Hagen is dating a Timpview girl and both Hagen and Pututau have several friends who go to Timpview.

In fact, during the day Mandy, Hagen's girlfriend from Timpview, gave him a surprise.

"After shootaround (Friday morning) she decorated my car. It said birds rule and dogs drool. She really wants us to lose tonight. I told her I would do anything for her and she said, 'I really want you to lose.' I told her anything but that," Hagen said. "Everyone has heard about us dating and they (Timpview) don't like it. They think she's a traitor, she's the enemy. I couldn't get her to cheer for me. She's through and through Timpview."

With the state tournament just a week away, Timpview has established itself as the clear 4A favorite. The T-Birds are ranked No. 1 in both the *Salt Lake Tribune* and the *Deseret News*. Olympus is ranked second and Provo, after losing its only game of the season to Timpview a few weeks ago, has dropped to third.

The attitude in the halls of Provo High this time is different. Students don't feel the same enthusiasm. Expectations are gone. Even Provo students have bought into the Timpview hype.

In the locker room before the game, the coaches make their last pitch to get the team fired up.

"They're No. 1 now. It's fun to be ranked No. 3. I don't even think your parents believe you can beat these guys," Schooney says. "The strength of their team are juniors and we're seniors, so let's go beat them. I want to kick their ass."

Now it's Drury's turn.

"I don't know what to say, if you're not ready. This is the type of game you dream about in high school. Go out and make something happen. I don't have too many more of these games left in my career, I'm going to enjoy this. You guys should have fun too. Let's take a moment."

Before the game begins, Timpview's Ryan Jackson is honored by McDonalds as a McDonalds All-American.

By the time the two teams take the floor at the Thunderdome, the gym looks like a snake after it just ate. The capacity is about 2,800 fans, but the Thunderdome is like a bowl, with a large walkaway above the highest row where fans can walk around the arena. Tonight people are packed five deep. The estimated crowd is 3,500.

From the start both Wesleys show they have come to play. Tai scores inside and is fouled to start the game, but a lane violation wipes out a chance for a three-point play. Ryan Shumpert scores for Timpview to tie the game. Tai scores again and is fouled, but once again, a lane violation erases a chance for a three-point play. After another Shumpert basket, Tika scores to give Provo a 6-4 lead, but then Timpview surges ahead with another bucket from Shumpert and one from Tanner Harmon.

Matt Pinegar runs down the clock for the last shot in the quarter. He's one-on-one with Hagen. He dribbles through his legs, fakes a drive to the basket and gets the separation he needs. He pulls up and drains a 17-foot jumper at the buzzer to give Timpview a 10-6 lead at the end of the quarter.

"I told you the team who gets the most shots will win. We've already had five turnovers," Drury says to his team between quarters.

Pututau shouts, "Let's get the ball inside to Tika."

Matt Mortensen hits a jumper to start the second quarter and gives Timpview a 12-6 lead. Tai scores inside to cut the lead to 12-8, but Mortensen strikes again and after an offensive foul on Hagen, Jackson hits two free throws to give the T-Birds a 16-8 lead.

But just when Timpview is beginning to pull away, Hagen scores his first points of the game on a jumper. Cory Carter comes off the bench to hit a 15-foot jumper.

Timpview's Brad Shumpert, the twin brother of Ryan, counters with a basket, but Carter comes back with a three-pointer to cut the lead to 18-15.

Provo finally catches Timpview at 21 when Hagen hits another jumper with a minute left in the half. Carter drops in two free throws to give the Bulldogs their first lead of the game at 23-21, but Jackson answers with a basket to leave the game tied at 23 at the half.

"I like the way we weathered the storm in a hostile environment," Drury says in the locker room. "We had five turnovers in the first half. Give those five possessions back and what would the score be?

"They don't like us right now. We're supposed to be 10 points behind right now. They are questioning it. Tai, you're kicking the crap out of (Chris) Miles. That's why he's not out there.

"One official told me out there that I can't say another word or I'll be tossed. Don't you let him take the game away from you.

"They're jumping our plays and we're jumping theirs. Now it's just a matter of who is tougher. This is your game."

In the third quarter, the powerful T-Birds begin to open up a lead once again. Pinegar scores and after a Hagen offensive foul, Ryan Shumpert scores again to give Timpview a 33-27 lead with 2:54 left in the third quarter. But Tika keeps Provo in the game. He hits two free throws and scores the final six points of the quarter for the

Bulldogs, but Ryan Shumpert responds with four points and Brad Shumpert adds a bucket to help the T-Birds take a 39-33 lead into the final quarter.

Timpview now has Provo right where it wants—on the ropes. Jackson scores to open the fourth quarter, giving Timpview a 41-33 lead, but just when the top-ranked T-Birds were ready to run away with the game, Provo finds a way to fight back.

Carter hits a jumper. Ryan Shumpert misses two free throws and is called for an offensive foul. Hagen then heats up. He hits his first three-pointer on the night and suddenly Timpview's lead is down to one at 41-40 with 4:50 left in the game.

Two minutes later, the Bulldogs have the lead when Tai hits two free throws to give Provo a 46-44 lead. Timpview then tries to run a new offense that Provo hadn't seen, but it backfires. Pututau deflects a pass and Stringham, who was out of position, turns out to be in the perfect position. He chases down and grabs the loose ball. Stringham misses the layup, but Tai gets the rebound and scores to give Provo a 48-44 lead with 2:06 left.

The see-saw game continues when Miles answers the call for Timpview by kissing a 10-footer off the glass. Hagen is fouled and sent to the line for two free throws. He makes the first one, but misses the second. Tai tries to grab the rebound, but is called for going over the back of Jackson, his fifth foul.

It doesn't look like Provo can pull off the upset without Tai. Jackson promptly makes Provo pay by hitting both free throws and trimming the lead to 49-48 with 1:31 left.

Drury senses the time is right for Provo to go into its motion offense. Make that its patient motion offense. If the Bulldogs take a shot, it better be a high-percentage one.

Unfazed by the pressure, Stringham posts up and scores inside, but Pinegar cashes in two free throws for Timpview to cut the lead back to one with 44 seconds remaining.

Timpview now must foul. The T-Birds chose Stringham, who steps up to the free-throw line for two shots with 28 seconds left.

Talk about state tournament type pressure. This is it. All the times Provo has come out on the wrong end of its game were against Timpview. Now the ball is in Stringham's hands. His first free throw hits the back of the rim and bounces away to the delight of the Timpview fans. His second free throw goes in and out.

Unbelievable. Timpview pulls down the rebound and now has a chance to go for the win.

But before the T-Birds can get off a shot, Hagen deflects a pass and Stringham comes up with the ball and quickly gives it back to Hagen, who is immediately fouled with 14 seconds left.

The pressure is back. The game is now in Hagen's hands. He has never beaten Timpview as a starter. Now he could blame no one but himself.

Timpview coach Perry Wildeboer calls a timeout.

When the players return to the court, Hagen steps to the free-throw line. Bounce, bounce, bounce. The shot is up.

Swish. Hagen is money.

Bounce, bounce, bounce. The shot is up.

Swish. Hagen is clutch.

Timpview still has hope, the T-Birds are only down three. Pinegar gets an open three and takes it, but his three-pointer is off the mark. The rebound goes out of bounds with one second left. The official rules the ball went off a Provo player.

Can you believe it?

The top-ranked T-Birds are not dead yet. But what kind of shot can you get with one second left and down three?

How about a three-pointer in the corner with the ball in the hands of the team's best shooter?

No one on Provo could explain how Mortensen was left all alone in the corner, but he was, and when the ball got into his hands, Mortensen got off a three-pointer before the horn sounded.

Will Provo finally have a win? Will Timpview's six-game winning streak (the longest ever against Provo) be snapped?

The shot was on line, but a little short. It bounced off the rim and in the air, igniting a Provo celebration. The Provo fans emptied the stands and swarmed the floor. Timpview fans quickly ran onto the floor to challenge Provo, but police separated the two schools from letting their fists settle the score.

A group of Provo students hoisted Tai up on their shoulders. The players are mobbed by their classmates. Stringham and Tika hold up

Tai Wesley is in the middle of a jubilant Provo crowd celebrating Provo's big win over No. 1 ranked Timpview.

their index fingers. "No. 1, baby!"

The joy, the sheer excitement, was unlike anything Provo had experienced before. The celebration continued for five minutes before they made their way to the locker room.

Inside the locker room, Stringham shouted, "Yeah! Oh, Yeah!"

Mercer whipped a towel in the air and shouted, "We finally got them!"

Hagen sat on the bench and beamed with excitement. Pututau smiled and in a higher voice than normal said, "Sweet!"

When the whole team finally gets into the locker room, Drury takes the stage. The players wait for their coach to speak.

It's all silence.

For 30 seconds not a word is spoken. Another 30 seconds passes while Drury tries to compose himself.

Tears are attacking his eyelids wanting to escape, but Drury won't let it happen.

"Coach (Keli), how many times in the 12 years you've been with me have you seen me cry?"

"None."

"That's one of the best efforts I've ever seen," Drury said. "You had two or three times where you could have walked away and still held your head up, you still could have said you tried, but you didn't. Craig misses two free throws, but then Joey gets his hand on the ball and you got the ball to Mick. I've never seen a better effort.

"I've coached a lot of great players, Mark Durrant, Jake Chrisman and a heck of a lot of other great players, but I've never seen a better effort than the way Tika played, I just can't contain it. I don't think I've seen anyone rebound better than Craig. Mick, I think you've sucked and so do some of you, but after you took it at him (Pinegar), it was great. I'm so proud of all of you. I could mention each one of you by name.

"Unfortunately this wasn't the state championship, was it? As much as we want it to be. Timpview is going to have a poster like we did if they're smart and they'll have it in their locker room like we did, and if we meet again they'll have that chip on their shoulder just like we did.

"I wish I could take this game, your attitude, and give it to your sons. They would be proud of you."

Schooney is next up. "Let's give it up for coach (Drury)."

The players give him a rousing applause.

"Everyone was working together. It was awesome," Schooney says.

The coaches leave the players to dress and celebrate and of course continue the Scrub Cup tradition.

"SCRUB CUP!" Snarr yells.

The players pound the orange lockers.

There is only one nominee tonight, but before the winner is announced, it's time for a few shoutouts.

"Give it up for coach Drury's sweet speech."

Another roar fills the room, undoubtedly heard by Timpview across the hall.

"We played such a sweet game and there weren't really any dumb plays, so there is just one nomination. Tai. When you grabbed the rebound and knocked (Jackson) to the floor."

Speech.

"This is my second one in a row, but I'm not really good at speeches," he says.

No one seems to mind that Tai's speech is weak.

When Hagen and Pututau come out of the locker room, they're wearing orange Timpview 6th man T-shirts, usually reserved for Timpview's diehard fans.

Finally, they have bragging rights.

Since there is no bus for the players to board, most of them will be driving home. The team bands together just in case there are some Timpview fans waiting in the parking lot.

In the other locker room, Timpview struggled to make some sense of the loss. What went wrong? How did it happen?

They had an eight-point lead in the fourth quarter. Timpview now felt like Provo had three weeks earlier.

The Bulldogs file out of the locker room. There they go into the night to celebrate the biggest win of their lives. The pressure is gone. There's one thought that won't let the smiles leave their faces. This win can never be taken away.

This is the pinnacle of the season. It's impossible for them to know at the time. High school kids don't think about it. When you're 16 or 17 years old, you don't think about defining moments of your life. The glass is full, or nearly full. Maybe just a sip is gone.

Winning will never feel this good unless they win a state championship. In fact, it's not likely they will ever feel this kind of emotion again.

"I haven't really felt like that before. It was a cool feeling. I don't even know how to describe it. I was so pumped up," Tika said, who led Provo with 14 points. "Cheerleaders were giving us hugs and some people lifted me up in the air. It's close to a state championship feeling. I just wanted to leave it on the floor. I knew it was the last time I would play in that gym."

When the weekend was over, the celebration continued after Monday's practice. The coaches take the Timpview Thunderstruck Poster to the parking lot where coach Keli brought a box of matches. The players take turns tearing up the poster and throwing the pieces of the poster onto the fire, officially cleansing their system of the Timpview loss.

Soon there is nothing left but black ashes. Pututau and Mercer scoop up some of the black ashes into a Gatorade cup and will keep it as a souvenir.

The poster was torched and their demons were exercised. With just one game left in the season, Provo was peaking. The Bulldogs had just got a taste of what winning a state championship would be like.

And there was nothing quite like it.

CHAPTER EIGHTEEN

HEADS WE WIN, TAILS YOU LOSE

The brackets for the state 4A high school tournament are out and there is one spot on the bracket that raises an instant red flag for Drury.

It is Region 6 No. 2. The second place team in Region 6 plays the fourth place team in Region 7 at 9:30 a.m. at the Dee Events Center in Ogden, an hour and a half bus ride, while the No. 1 seed plays at a more reasonable hour—5:50 p.m. against Region 5's fourth-place team.

No one wants the earlier game—the opening game of the tournament. It's too early. To get through the rush hour traffic and get to Ogden in time, Drury figures he'd have to leave at around 6 a.m., which means the players would have to get up about 5 a.m.

No thanks.

The other option is to take the team to Ogden on Sunday night and stay in a hotel. It's what most Utah County teams have done in the past and it's what Drury decides he will do if Provo ends up with the second seed from Region 6.

With that in mind, Drury and Timpview coach Perry Wildeboer don't want to wait for the outcome of Tuesday's game to break the tie. There are hotel reservations to make and more importantly, both coaches want to know where they'll end up so they can scout their first-round opponent.

Both teams still have one game left on Tuesday, but that's not expected to matter. Provo plays at American Fork, while Timpview ends at Spanish Fork. Both teams should have little trouble finishing off region play with a win.

Since Provo and Timpview are tied at 8-1 in region play, and the two teams split their season series, a coin flip will have to decide who gets the No. 1 seed.

So Monday morning, the first day back to school after Provo's upset of Timpview, Drury and Schoonover meet Wildeboer and his assistant Nate Warner to take care of the coin flip.

"Who wants to call it," said Timpview assistant principal Brand Monks.

Drury wants to call it, but hesitates to say anything. So he says, "Let's let Jeff call it."

It's agreed.

Schooney gets the call.

Monks flips a quarter in the air.

Schoonover calls out, "Heads."

Heads it is.

Provo at 19-1 overall, will represent Region 6 as the No. 1 seed from the region, while Timpview 18-2 overall, will take the second seed from Region 6.

The way the pieces have fallen into place, this must be a season of destiny.

Now Provo will play at 5:50 on Monday night, but there is a downside to the draw. Provo will get either East or Highland. East was a Final Four team last year and the Leopards had most of their players back from last year.

Highland has made a habit of peaking late. Last year Provo opened the tournament against Highland. The Rams upset Provo in the first round and went on to to win the state tournament.

Both East and Highland figure to be a tougher draw than Mountain View, or whoever ends up with the fourth spot from Region 7, but the road looks easier the rest of the way.

"I think there are two pros to the one seed, and one pro to the two seed," Drury explained. "The disadvantage of No. 1 seed is you could play East in the first round. I think East could beat anybody. If East doesn't get it, I'll be ticked, because then it really will be an easier road."

Then after a pause, Drury adds, "There might be a secret surprise in the two seed."

In other words, Confucius say, "He who tries to predict bracket strength often learns valuable lesson—be careful what you wish for."

Drury sends freshman coach Don Johnson to scout Highland on Tuesday night instead of coming to the team's game against American Fork.

It turns out Johnson missed a game the team will be talking about for the rest of the season.

This is it. Provo at American Fork, the final regular season game of the season. It's Tuesday afternoon at 5 p.m. and the team is spread out in the balcony bleachers doing their own thing during the JV game.

Hagen is writing poetry to Mandy, his girlfriend from Timpview. He takes a break to talk about the future.

"Before, I had never beaten Timpview as a starter and never won a state tournament game. I got the Timpview one, now it's time to take care of the second one," Hagen said. "Coach Drury tells me that people always ask him how good of a point guard I am and he says, 'He's great, but he's never won a state tournament game.' Then he tells me, 'You don't want to be mentioned that way do you?' That's a lot of pressure, but that's okay with me."

The other players listen to music or talk to cheerleaders with little to worry about. This game should just be a formality.

American Fork comes into the game in disarray. The team center Stefan Zimmerman, who committed to play at Utah as a junior, and was kicked off the team for verbally abusing the coaches.

Zimmerman had served a pair of one-game suspensions before head coach Doug Meacham decided Zimmerman had to go.

Zimmerman started his career at Orem as a freshman, then transferred to Mountain View for his sophomore and junior years. He left Mountain View when he felt like first-year coach Jason Young didn't get him involved in the offense enough.

If the Zimmerman situation wasn't bad enough, the team's captains Taylor Brown and Zach Adamson were suspended two games for violating team rules. The Provo game was their second of the two-game suspension.

Playing Provo without three key starters figured to be an impossible task—this had the makings of a massacre.

American Fork's slim hopes rest on senior Bo Fowler and a trio of talented sophomores in Rick and James Shoff and Brenan Davis.

Fowler had taken a back seat in the scoring department, but tonight American Fork needed him to lead the Cavemen.

Before tip-off Drury warns the team that American Fork has nothing to lose. The Cavemen have already locked up third place in Region 6 and a playoff spot, regardless of what happens.

The prophet Jeremiah was back, warning his players to bring their A game.

But once again, no one listened.

It took about two minutes for Provo to find out it was in trouble. Fowler leads the Cavemen to a 9-4 first-quarter lead. After just two minutes Stringham picks up his third foul and heads to the bench, but Pututau responds with back-to-back threes to give Provo a 10-9 lead. It doesn't last long because someone has hit the snooze button on Provo's defense.

When American Fork's Mitch Beck scores, he gives the Cavemen a 11-10 lead at the end of the quarter.

It's only been one quarter, but American Fork is sensing it can play with Provo. The Cavemen are beginning to believe in themselves.

The Bulldogs take a brief 19-15 lead after a Tika basket and another Pututau three-pointer, but the problem continues to be defense. American Fork spreads out the floor and begins cutting backdoor for easy layups.

Fowler hits a three-pointer, but is then called for an offensive foul, his third of the game. American Fork receives another blow. One of the team's best shooters, Kyle Fillmore sprains his ankle and leaves the game for good. Now it's just a matter of time before Provo pulls away. American Fork's top five players are not on the floor.

But none of that matters to sophomore Rick Shoff. He's been waiting for a chance to prove he can play against the best team in Utah.

Shoff scores six of American Fork's next eight points to give the Cavemen a 26-25 lead.

A player on Provo's bench mumbles, "We're losing to a bunch of sophomores."

American Fork sophomore Clayton Searle put the finishing

touches on the first half when he scores to give American Fork a 28-25 lead at intermission.

It was now clear Provo made a huge mistake. The Bulldogs had allowed American Fork to stay in the game and now the Cavemen had all the momentum they needed.

Before Drury address the team in the locker room, he stays outside with his coaches to vent. "I don't know what to say. This is not the same team I coached last week."

Drury then opens the locker room door and scowls at his players.

"You tell me 'I know I made a mistake coach.' Well then quit making mistakes! I don't think I've seen you give them the ball and let them go make a layup, but the way you're playing, I expect to see that in the second half.

"I'm mystified why you would come out and lay an egg. They are using the whole floor. I don't mind the 25 points, but you've given up 28 points to a mediocre team…You're prima donnas, you're arrogant. Maybe you have dates tonight, maybe you're going roller skating and you're not interested in playing this game. There's nothing I can say but X's and O's. You've got to get them behind so they have to attack and not spread the floor."

Schoonover tries to breath some life into the team by reminding them what's at stake.

"This is for the No. 1 seed and for a region championship. You've got to go out and want it."

A loss would negate all that Provo gained by winning at Timpview, and no team wants to go into the state tournament on a losing note.

With that in mind, Provo takes the floor in the third quarter with a renewed resolve and are promptly torched by layups from Fowler and Beck. Another easy basket from Fowler gives American Fork a 34-25 lead and prompts a Provo timeout.

During the timeout Drury tells Tai, "I can't play you, if you're not going to play defense. They've just got three layups."

Drury goes with a smaller lineup, but it doesn't work either. American Fork continues to score at will on Provo's vaunted defense.

Fowler scores seven points in the quarter and when Searle adds two free throws, suddenly American Fork's lead is 41-29.

Stringham powers inside for a layup to cut the lead to 41-31 at the end of the third quarter, but by now Provo knows it's on the ropes.

The fourth quarter begins just like the start of every quarter, with an American Fork run. Beck and Fowler each score to give the Cavemen their biggest lead of the game at 45-31.

American Fork is now the teacher and Provo is the student. Class is in session. Today's topic is, "You can't turn it on and off."

The one hope for Provo is the youthful Cavemen will wilt under the pressure down the stretch.

A Hagen three-pointer cuts the lead to 47-39 with 3:43 left in the game, but Shoff answers with a three-point play. Drury calls on freshman Kenyon Koop, who gets his first meaningful minutes of the year.

Koop is called for traveling. Tika then scores to cut the lead to 50-41 with three minutes remaining, but Provo's comeback is facing two big road blocks. American Fork is now in the double bonus so the Cavemen will shoot two free throws every time Provo commits a foul, and the Bulldogs can't force a turnover.

A Corbin Mercer offensive rebound basket gives Provo hope with 1:15 left. The American Fork lead is down to six at 55-49.

Fowler responds by hitting four free throws, but Tika scores inside and Cory Carter pops a three, cutting the lead to 59-54 with 24 seconds left.

The Bulldogs need a stop and they need it now. Instead, Provo is forced to foul sophomore Brenan Davis, who hits both free throws with 18 seconds remaining. A quick Hagen three-pointer gives Provo one last chance. The Bulldogs now trail by just four at 61-57, but there's just 10 seconds left. Provo needs a miracle.

Instead, American Fork's Shay Conder is immediately fouled and he hits two free throws to seal the upset. American Fork fans begin the chant, "Overrated, overrated."

Stringham hits a three-pointer, but it's too late. Time runs out on Provo. In a stunning upset, American Fork hangs on for a 63-60 win. Considering the circumstances, it is one of the biggest upsets of the season.

A stunned Provo team gathers up its warmups and heads to the locker room where American Fork students are lined up to rub it in.

They shake their keys as the players walk by. It's their way of saying goodbye.

"Basketball is not a simple game. You can't just go out there and play one-on-one. If you could, the best player would win every time. Sometimes it's style versus style. I would like to thank American Fork. I hoped you learned something...If you play like that next Monday (at the state tournament) you'll be through at 11:15.

"If you don't have confidence in what we're telling you as coaches, if you don't believe in what we're telling you then I might as well get my golf clubs out now.

"I think you guys wanted to miss school on Monday because you sucked. You were arrogant and cocky. You didn't think they could beat you. You are a very good team, but anyone can beat you. This team might have helped you win a state championship if you learned something."

Drury went up and down the lineup. If Stringham was rebounding like he did against Timpview, he wouldn't have had three quick fouls. Tai has to play better defense. Tika has to demand the ball. Hagen has to leave his passive game at home. Corbin needs to get the job done earlier.

Everyone can take blame for this loss.

Coach Keli says, "The biggest mistake we made as coaches was telling you we won the flip. It's a good thing there is snow out there, because I would send the bus home and you would have to find yourself a ride."

Schoonover adds, "I talked to one of our girl basketball players today and she told me she was glad they lost (in the girls state tournament) because she was sick of basketball. I wanted to strangle her. This is what you practice for all year to get to this point. I watched Wasatch win the 3A state title and hoist their point guard on their shoulders and everyone was chanting, 'Cottle, Cottle.' I want that for you Mick. You've got to go get your name on a trophy and hoist it into the air and experience that great feeling."

The win has given American Fork life. American Fork assistant coach Tim LaComb says the team's 14-7 record is a lot like another team last year. LaComb coached at Lone Peak last year when the Knights made it to the state championship game with a 14-7 record.

"Our kids are resilient. It's what keeps a guy coaching," said American Fork head coach Doug Meacham. "Coach Drury is a class guy. He knew we had to play close to a perfect game to win. All season, we've never had a game where we had less than 10 turnovers. Tonight we had just four. They're going to be a team to be reckoned with at the state tournament."

The regular season ends for Provo at 19-2. On the day the Bulldogs were ranked No. 1 once again, they lost and they'll now head into the state tournament to play a familiar foe: Orem, Provo's old rival.

CHAPTER NINETEEN

THE END OF THE JOURNEY

It's time to get serious. This is what it's all about. This is the biggest week of their lives. All of those basketball camps, summer games, three-hour practices.

All those times running stairs in the old gym, lifting weights in the summer, and playing basketball year-around. The years of preparation have all been aimed at one week—the week of the state tournament.

And it's finally here.

Thanks to the American Fork loss, it's here a little sooner than expected. The players meet Sunday at 4:30 p.m. at Provo High School in preparation of their 9:30 a.m. game Monday morning to open the state tournament.

All the players are on board except one. After a 10 minute wait for junior guard Jordan Snarr, the the bus pulls out and coach Keli shows the players a surprise he's made for them.

It's another poster, like the one he made after the Timpview loss.

"American Fork sophomore/JV team beats No. 1 ranked Provo."

There are two other signs on the bus that say, "Good Luck at State," but coach Keli isn't ready to let the lesson of American Fork go. He makes sure all of the players see his poster.

The team opts to stay at the LaQuinta Inn in Layton, about 15 minutes from the Dee Events Center.

Drury has already gone over a few of the rules. No one is to go in the pool or hot tub and absolutely, without question, the lights will go out early. Everyone is to be in their rooms by 10 p.m.

A late night would defeat the purpose of staying in Layton.

Once the players get to their rooms, they all begin to scatter.

There is time to get some dinner at one of the surrounding restaurants before the team meeting begins at 7 p.m. in the hotel conference room.

Drury and coach Keli have brought up their own dinner, a giant sub sandwich. They offer to share with any of the players or other coaches, but most opt for restaurant food.

At the 7 p.m. meeting, Drury tells the team, "This is your best chance to win a state championship (aimed at the younger players). Right now you're 19-2 and in the driver's seat to win it. You've won the tournament in Hawaii, you were undefeated in preseason play, and 8-2 in the toughest region in the state. You deserve to be where you are."

Coach Keli then takes over. He hands out what he calls a survivor kit. It's a ziplock bag full of different items like a toothpick, a rubber band, a Band-Aid, a pencil, an eraser, a piece of gum, and a mini candy bar.

Along with the ziplock bag is a 5x7 piece of green paper that explains what the items in the survival kit are for.

Toothpick: Will remind you to pick out the strengths in others.

Rubber band: Will remind you to be flexible and that all things can be worked out.

Band-Aid: Will remind you to heal hurt feelings, your own or maybe a team members.

Pencil: Will remind you to list goals and priorities for ever game.

Eraser: Will remind you that everyone makes mistakes, so lift each other up.

Gum: Will remind you to stick with the task at hand.

Gold Nugget (mini candy bar): Will remind you that you are worth your weight in gold and that you can accomplish anything.

Coach Keli then asks the players to write down three things they can do to help the team win.

He then asks, "Are you a survivor? Are you going to survive poor officiating? Are you going to come up with a loose ball?"

Drury then shares an e-mail he received from a former player after Provo's win over Timpview.

Robbie Holcombe, who is in Africa serving a church mission, heard about Provo's big win and sent Drury this message.

"As you go to state remember to stay focused, play each minute harder than you played the last minute. Square up and shoot the lights out, but remember it's defense that will ultimately get you the prize. Bring home the state banner. Good luck. Go Dogs!"

Holcombe then added a poem he wrote that he hoped would make an impact on the team.

The worst feeling I ever had was when I lost something I should have won.
It was right there waiting to be grabbed, too afraid was I to reach for some.
Of the glory that was mine, it mocked me then departed out of sight,
and after that I could not find for it was gone, up and took flight.
So now I prepare for when opportunity knocks, hoping it will come to me again.
If there is a next time of which we talk, I'm ready to make opportunity my friend.
Once in a while everyone has their chance for greatness, I'm going to take mine and make it last.

Holcombe's thoughts are not uncommon; former players often come back to visit Drury and wish they could go back and do it again.

When former player B.J. Chandler (1994) visited practice the week before the state tournament, he reflected back on his playing days. He shook his head as he watched practice, "If I could only do it over again, I would go all out at practice..."

Time tends to give former players a change in their vision, a new prescription. The strategy, the plays drawn up in the huddle, and those pregame thoughts written on the chalkboard for some reason are not usually comprehended until years later. Then one day, when playing in a city league game, they have a startling revelation. They would finally say to themselves, "I get it now."

The voices from the past give the players something to think about, even if it's just a passing thought.

After all, what does someone else's laments of years ago have anything to do with me?

The team gets up at 6:30 a.m. and walks across the street to

Cracker Barrel restaurant where Drury has already pre-ordered their breakfast. Two pancakes and an egg and juice.

After breakfast, the team meets one more time before they board the bus.

"This will be one of the funnest weeks of your life," Drury says. "I promise you, you'll never forget this week. You will take this to your grave."

The Dee Events Center is empty when the players arrive. They quickly dress so they can start shooting and get used to the arena.

When it's time to go into the locker room, Drury offers one last thought.

"They are excited about the American Fork loss," he says. "They believe they're better than American Fork. They feel like they can get you."

Now for a little shot of confidence.

"We deserve to win this game. They are 9-11. They don't deserve to win this, but they'll take it. They've got to win one game and it will make their season," Drury says. "You've got to respect them, but I do believe if we get up on them, they'll lay down, but they won't do it without a push.

"I think you're ready. I think you've learned your lesson. Thank you American Fork. If you took a poll and asked who was a better team, Provo or Orem, 100 percent would say you guys. Let's play like it. Let's play the best we can play. Let's take a minute."

The players kneel down in prayer or meditation, just minutes away from playing the biggest game of their lives.

When the Bulldogs take the floor, they notice Provo students outnumber Orem students two to one. Apparently Orem fans aren't as optimistic as Provo fans.

Finally, the game is underway and Orem's Johnny Nielsen is called for an offensive foul. Nielsen then comes up with a steal, but Orem promptly turns the ball over. Tai scores inside for the first basket of the game with 7:05 left in the first quarter to give Provo a 2-0 lead.

Brooks Christiansen comes up with a steal for Orem. Lincoln Reid pulls down an offensive rebound and is fouled. He makes both free throws to tie the game. Mat Taylor then scores for Orem to put the Tigers up 4-2. Hagen then turns the ball over, which prompts a Provo timeout.

Three minutes into the quarter and Provo has just two points. This is not the battle plan to get Orem to surrender.

"Get the ball MOVING!" Drury shouts above the sounds of the band playing during the timeout.

Christiansen, Orem's point guard, has come to play. He scores back-to-back baskets coming out of the Provo timeout. Tai counters to cut the lead to 8-4.

But Mike Gilbert scores and is fouled. He hits a free throw to convert a three-point play to give the Tigers an 11-4 lead with three minutes left in the quarter.

Despite the deficit, Provo fans know there's no need to panic. It's early. There's a lot of ball to be played and Provo is playing like it. The sense of urgency hasn't checked out of the hotel yet.

Tai is fouled inside, but he misses both free throws and is then called for an over the back foul on the rebound. Orem follows with a turnover, which leads to a pair of buckets from Tika to cut the lead to 11-8. But the Bulldogs quickly fall behind again. Reid scores and after a Hagen turnover, Christiansen drains a 22-foot three pointer at the buzzer to give Orem a stunning 16-8 lead at the end of the first quarter.

Christiansen's shot sends Orem's bench and their fans into a frenzy. After one quarter, they are dominating Provo, their oldest rival, and a team that's been ranked No. 1 for a good part of the year.

Convinced that the first quarter is a fluke, Provo fans can still be seen smiling. They know it's just a matter of time before the Bulldogs blow this team away.

The second quarter begins with Tai scoring four quick points, but Reid answers with four points of his own. Nielsen then comes up with a steal, which leads to a pair of Reid free throws.

Orem's Scott Smith then scores to give the Tigers their biggest lead of the game at 24-12 with five minutes left in the half.

Tai is called for another offensive foul and even though Cory Carter and Hagen come up with steals, the Bulldogs still can't score.

Orem's Tom Fredricksen buries a three-pointer at the buzzer to send Orem into the locker room with a 27-14 lead.

Provo closes the half without scoring a single point for the last 4:43.

What in the world is happening?

The American Fork loss was supposed to prevent this kind of performance.

How could a team that was under .500 on the year be dominating a team they lost to in the regular season?

Welcome to the high school state tournament, where upsets can happen and often do.

Predictably, Drury is fuming. No one is safe from his wrath.

"There's not a damn thing I can do for you. Mick, there is a reason why you haven't won a state tournament game as our point guard. It's like you're too damn good to hustle."

As the point guard, Hagen usually takes most of the heat, but he's hardly alone.

"Joey you look good in your uniform. We could take a picture of you.…We're 0-5 from the three-point line, Cory, shoot the basketball for us when you're open and knock down some three's."

Drury then focuses on Provo's big men. Orem is doubling and tripling the Wesleys and trying to force a turnover before they can pass out of the triple-team.

"You've got to be strong inside. They're waiting for you to put the ball on the floor."

There are many areas of concern. Drury can't get to them all, but he still tries.

"We didn't get a rebound until two minutes to go in the first quarter. When they shoot, they get it back. They've taken 20 shots to our 16 and the turnovers are ridiculous. We have 10 turnovers. You're total aggression is gone. I don't know where it went."

The halftime stats make a case for Drury's argument. Provo shot 54 percent from the field, but were 0 for 5 from the three-point line.

Most alarming for Provo was Orem's shooting percentage. The Tigers were on fire. They shot a sizzling 73 percent.

But Provo still believes Orem will cool off and if there's one bright spot for Provo, the Bulldogs believe they can't possibly play this bad in the second half.

The third quarter begins with a statement from Tai. He grabs an offensive rebound and scores. A goal tending call gives Orem a basket, but Tai answers with another basket off an offensive rebound. Pututau then deflects an Orem pass and Stringham picks up the loose ball. The Bulldogs run. Hagen pulls up for a three. It's good.

Drury raises his hands to signal the Provo comeback. The Orem lead is down to 29-21. The Bulldogs have started the third quarter on a 7-1 run.

But Nielsen puts the brakes on Provo's run. He scores inside, then follows with a three-pointer to push the Tiger lead back to 34-21. Tika answers with a basket and Pututau comes up with another steal, but Hagen misses a three-pointer, and on Orem's next possession, Reid finds an open seem in Provo's defense and drives down the lane for a thundering one-hand dunk.

Nielsen gets loose again. He cashes in on a three-point play and Reid gets the ball on a fastbreak and scores on a rim-rocker, a two handed dunk, to give Orem a 41-25 lead with 1:24 left in the third quarter.

Drury calls on backup guard Kade Koop to give the team a spark, and he responds with a basket to stop Orem's 12-4 run. But Koop's basket still leaves Provo down 41-25 at the end of the third quarter.

It's gut check time for Provo. Eight minutes left in the game. For the seniors, eight minutes left in most of their basketball careers.

It's do or die.

Hagen opens the fourth quarter with a three-pointer to cut the lead to 41-28. You knew Provo would make a run sometime. It was just a matter of when.

Pututau comes up with a steal and gets the ball to Hagen, who quickly fires another three, but he misses.

Nielsen is ready to make Provo pay. He comes up with a three-point play for Orem, but Tika keeps Provo close with a basket. The Bulldogs now have no choice but to put on a full-court press with the hope they can force some turnovers to get back in the game.

Christiansen is fouled. He makes one of two free throws. Koop counters with a hoop for Provo to cut the Orem lead to 45-32 with 6:09 left in the game. Nielsen misses the front end of 1-and-1, but every time Provo catches a break, the Bulldogs can't cash in on it.

Hagen's crosscourt pass is picked off by Christiansen. Pututau fouls him to prevent a layup, picking up his fourth foul of the game. Christiansen hits both free throws and after a Provo miss, Nielsen hits a pair of free throws.

It's official, there is now a lump of the throat of the Provo players, while Orem fans begin chanting "Overrated, overrated."

Provo fans are powerless to counter. Orem has the scoreboard and that's all that matters.

Pututau hits a jumper and Stringham comes up with a steal. Tika then scores inside at the five-minute mark to trim the lead to 49-36.

The Bulldogs have three legitimate three-point shooters, so there is still hope, but Orem begins to pull away with free throws. The Tigers push their lead to 56-38 with 3:20 left in the game, before Provo starts its final run.

Koop hits a three-pointer.

And? And nothing. That's it. That is Provo's run.

The run Orem feared never came. Christiansen breaks the press and scores on a layup. Gilbert makes one of two free throws for Orem and Koop grabs an offensive rebound and scores. Even though Orem misses its next four free throws, Provo is powerless to launch a comeback. There's just 1:50 left in the game and Provo can't shoot. When the Bulldogs make a three-pointer it seems like it's an accident.

The Bulldogs have waited too long. Orem leads 59-43.

Orem fans are talking again.

"Warm up the bus. Warm up the bus."

Pututau fouls out with 1:36 left in the game. Steve Torkildson takes his place. Scott Ady checks in with 1:28 left in the game, fulfilling his prediction. He said he would come back and he did.

Reid then puts the finishing touches off on the game when he thunders inside for a one-handed dunk.

The final score is a shocking, a 66-45 Orem win.

The win is shocking enough, but by 21 points?

The box score reveals the breakdown.

For starters, Provo had 18 turnovers. The Bulldogs shot 40 percent from the field and a forgettable 15 percent from the three-point line. Provo hit just 3 of 22 three-pointers.

Hagen was 2 for 9, Pututau was 0 for 6, Carter was 0 for 3.

Tika Wesley led the team with 14 points on 6 of 6 shooting, but he also had eight turnovers trying to pass out of double and triple teams.

Tai scored 12 points on 6 of 7 shooting from the field. Kade Koop is next on the team in scoring. He was a pleasant surprise. Koop, a rarely used junior, hit 4 of 5 shots. Hagen finished with just six points on 2 of 13 shooting. Pututau and Carter had just two points each and combined to shoot 2 for 12 from the field.

As a team, Provo's offense sputtered and misfired all game and turned in its worst outing of the year. The team's poor offensive effort rubbed off at the other end of the court on defense.

"There's been many games where I didn't think we'd score 20 points against them. Never in my wildest dreams did I think we could score 65 points on them," said a jubilant Orem coach Greg Sheidi. "I thought if we won it would be something like 41-37. In practice we would make 8-10 passes before we took a shot—we worked on being patient. It works if you can get a lead on them. If you don't then they won't come out and guard you."

Once again Provo had run into a hot team and for the third straight year lost in the first round of the state tournament. It's been a puzzling problem for Drury.

"I have a lot of respect for Provo. They have been the best program in the state in the last 25 years," Sheide added. "We tried to look at film and figure out how to score. Most teams can't score against them."

Sheide must have figured it out because Orem shot 68 percent from the field for the game—unheard of against Provo's defense.

Reid, Orem's explosive forward, led the Tigers with 21 points on 7 of 7 shooting from the field. Christiansen added 16 points including 7 of 10 free throws while Nielsen (4 for 4) added 14 for the Tigers.

The cheering from Orem's jubilant locker room can be heard from the door of Provo's locker room, which is like a viewing at a funeral home. The only talking that is done is in whispers and the only sounds are sporadic sniffles as players try to hold in the tears.

Drury finally breaks the silence.

"I'm proud of you as a team, but I don't think I could be more disappointed," Drury said in a quiet locker room.

"We played with no sense of urgency from the beginning of the game. You had a great year and I know it hurts that they didn't just beat us, they thrashed you," Drury adds. "But not too many people thought this team would be 19-3."

Coach Keli takes his turn. "This game is like the game of life. Pick up and learn from it. One of these days you might embrace the things we talked about and maybe you'll be e-mailing us like Robby Holcombe or B.J. Chandler. You lost your focus and your will to win. You didn't survive the battle."

The loss was especially emotional for Schooney, who began coaching when the seniors were freshmen.

"You guys are like part of my family. You (seniors) are the first group I've coached all the way through. I love each one of you. I wish you could have gone out on top. You deserved to."

As is the tradition, Drury lets his seniors say something before the team leaves the locker room.

"This is my fourth time (losing in the state tournament) and this sucks," Corbin said. "I've learned a lot about basketball in the last four years and more about life that I will never forget."

The seniors continue to speak.

"I love you coaches. It's been a fun four years, but it sucks having to end this way," Hagen says. "I still loved every minute of it. We've got the greatest coaches in Utah and the greatest people. Always work hard and have fun. I love you guys."

Now it's Tika's turn. The big post player who plays so hard has everyone's attention."You guys need to listen to the coaches, they know what they're talking about," Tika said. The emotion of the season then surfaced and Tika broke down in tears.

"I hate this feeling. This is the fourth time. Start working hard and do what you have to do to be successful."

Pututau, Stringham, and Ady offer up their thoughts and the players take turns saying goodbye to each other with hugs and tears.

The locker room scene ends with tradition. Drury wraps it up the way he always does.

"Let's take a minute if you want to."

The season is officially over.

The players make their way to the stands at the Dee Event Center and watch the other games until it's time to go. When everyone is out of the locker room, the Bulldogs board the bus and begin the long, somber ride home.

With the game over, Drury wonders to himself if he could have done something different.

"I wish I would have communicated that they didn't have to get it inside on the first pass. They could have gone inside and have it kicked back out and gone back inside, make 8-10 passes."

Drury sits in his usual spot on the bus, the second seat from the front. He pulls out a crossword puzzle to help take his mind off what just happened.

No. 7 down—a 10 letter word for a gut-wrenching loss—depression.

Laura and Val, the two stat girls, who are always a pleasant distraction, don't say a word.

Donnie, the trainer, reads the scriptures. The always upbeat Brad Corbitt is doing his best LaVell Edwards impression. Not even a BYU football victory could make him smile.

Well, maybe a win over Utah.

Joey rests his head back on the seat and closes his eyes. The tears have cleared off Tika's eyes. He tries to escape under the headphones of his music.

Corbin stares out the window of the bus.

The juniors know this isn't the end. The pain they feel is different. "Next year will be different. When I'm a senior . . ."

For the juniors, sophomores, or even the freshmen, this isn't the end. No matter what anyone else says, no e-mail from the past, no former player's lament can get through. Their thought process is a constant busy signal. They have another year.

Only when they are seniors can they look back and ask, "What if?"

The only teacher they will listen to is experience—their own.

Two days after the loss to Orem, the seniors are still moping around the hallway with all the energy of someone who has mono.

They've been asked the same question a hundred times.

"What happened?"

They all offered up slightly different answers, but the general consensus is the team got complacent, the team lost its edge.

"At the first of the season we had something to prove," Stringham said. "By the end of the year when we were ranked No. 1 or No. 2, I think we relaxed."

Another theory many of the players subscribe to has to do with the Timpview win.

"We all thought our main goal was to beat Timpview. Once that was done we thought, 'Okay we've succeeded now,'" Mercer explained. "That's not why we play basketball, not to just beat Timpview. We play basketball to win a state championship."

On a Wednesday, two days after Provo's state tournament exit, while the state tournament is going, Drury holds a players meeting in the afternoon. All the freshman, sophomores, and juniors who were in the program sit down in the team room, while Drury talks about next year.

When the meeting is over, Drury talks to Schooney and together they wonder aloud how they can possibly win with this group. They don't shoot real well, they're not a great rebounding group, and they have little varsity experience.

As coaches, they say that every year. But by March, by the end of the season, a transition happens. The makeover is complete. A season in Provo High School's basketball program has transformed them into better players, and at the same time, without even sensing the change, they have emerged as better people.

Better off than they would have been had they not played and prepared more for their next opponent.

Life.

Provo coach Craig Drury talks to the team during halftime of a game in the team room.

AFTERWORD

After Orem beat Provo, the Tigers went on to beat Roy, who came up with the other big upset of the first day when Roy stunned Olympus.

It just made the path for Timpview a little easier. Timpview won the state championship. The school's fifth state title since Provo High School's boundaries were divided and Timpview opened its doors in 1977.

Hagen, Pututau, and Tika Wesley, all played one more game. *The Daily Herald* All-Star Classic.

I was the coach. They helped me snap a seven-year losing streak. Wesley was the MVP of the game. He led the team with 15 points and was a finalist in the slam dunk competition. Hagen scored 13 points and Pututau added 8 points.

Tika was a First Team All-State selection and Hagen was named Second Team All-State.

Hagen represented Provo High School as its Sterling Scholar in Computer Technology and won the state Sterling Scholar award in Computer Technology and received a $1,000 check.

In Utah, there were 674 students competing for Sterling Scholars honors in 13 different categories, ranging from dance to math, from English to Science. An overall winner was chosen from each category. Then, the winners from each category compete against each other for the overall honors.

Drum roll please. The overall winner is . . . Mick Hagen. Yep, Hagen pocketed another honor and another check, this time for $1,500.

After he won Sterling Scholar honors, Hagen was asked to play soccer when the soccer team had several players either injured or academically ineligible. Hagen hadn't played soccer since the 8th grade, but he turned out to have a remarkable season. He scored 12 goals and helped Provo to the 4A state semifinals to Mountain View. He was named First-Team All-State.

Hagen turned 19 in May and was accepted to Princeton, where he's still undecided on whether or not he will play basketball. He has two years to think about it, because he accepted a call to Brazil to serve a two-year church mission.

Pututau plans on going to BYU after he serves a church mission to Mexico. He broke up with his wife, i.e. girlfriend.

Stringham picked up his baseball glove and joined Dustin Miggliacci, who quit the team in February, to concentrate on baseball. Stringham outdueled Springville High School ace pitcher Aaron Jensen, who was drafted and signed with the Seattle Mariners. Stringham helped Provo beat Springville and hand Jensen the only loss of his high school career.

Stringham was all-state honorable mention in baseball and left in early June for Northern California, where he planed on playing summer baseball and going to De Anza Junior College in Cupertino, California.

Tai Wesley packed his summer schedule with basketball tournaments. He played in California, Nevada, Nebraska, Washington, and North Carolina. The team he played with took second in a tournament in Las Vegas. One of their wins was over a loaded California all-star team. In November he verbally committed to play at BYU.

Steve Torkildson is attending Utah Valley State College where he is thinking of going into business.

Corbin Mercer was a regular at Provo's baseball games and spent the summer working and saving up for his church mission.

Ady began playing volleyball and was selected to play with the team representing Utah in the Goodwill Games in Russia in July. He is working and preparing to serve a church mission.

Coach Corbitt was a regular at BYU baseball games where he could be heard talking about BYU's upcoming football season. He decided not to come back for another season. Instead, he will concentrate on school.

Schooney moved to Cedar City, Utah for the summer to work on his master's degree. It's a program that takes two years. He returned to Provo for another year, but once he gets into administration, his coaching days will be over.

Coach Keli spent the summer season working at basketball camps at BYU, Utah State, and Provo High School. In the fall he returned to help Provo volleyball coach Wendy Bills for the 15th straight year.

Cory Green, the sophomore coach, was named the head coach of the girls team.

That left Drury to supervise open gym. On most afternoons Drury sat in a chair or on one of the bleacher benches and kept a watchful eye on his future.

He also married off his daughter, who married a man who had a child from a previous relationship. Of course, it was a girl.

Provo played in a spring tournament where the Bulldogs went 4-1. The highlight of the tournament was Cory Carter. Provo trailed by nine with 40 seconds left, but Carter scored 11 points in the final 40 seconds to help the Bulldogs pull out a stunning win.

"I've never seen anything like it," Schoonover said. "It was incredible."

As for the rest of the Bulldogs, they can be seen playing in the gym on a Wednesday afternoon or a Saturday morning. They practice and play year-round, preparing for another year *Under the Green Banners*.

0 26575 77549 5